CW00920026

# Write Useful Books

## Books

A modern approach to
*designing* and *refining*
recommendable nonfiction

by Rob Fitzpatrick
robfitz.com, rob@robfitz.com

version 1.02
writeusefulbooks.com

# CHAPTER 1

# What this guide is and isn't, how it can help you, and who I am

Writing a nonfiction book is a wonderful project, allowing you to preserve and share the most important things you've ever learned. Plus, a successful book will improve your reputation, your career, your earnings, and the lives of your readers.

Up until fairly recently, it was possible to receive at least some of these benefits by writing *any* book, regardless of its quality. But today, a million new titles are published per year and it's no longer enough to simply join the pile. Instead, you must create something that is able to stand out and succeed. And the most reliable path toward that goal — especially for an unproven author who lacks a pre-existing audience — is to write a book so startlingly useful that readers can't stop talking about it.

This guide proposes a different way of planning, writing, testing, and refining nonfiction, adapted from the hard-won lessons of product designers and entrepreneurs. When applied properly, it leads to books that can grow organically via reader recommendations for many years, without relying on either heavy marketing or a large author platform.

Our focus is squarely on the process and product of nonfiction books. For advice about writing the prose itself, I recommend *On Writing Well*, by William Zinsser. You'll find that book to be an extremely helpful complement to this one.

A major theme of this guide is to stop writing your manuscript in secret and start exposing it to — and learning from — real readers as quickly as possible. That might feel scary, but there are ways to do it safely, and it's worth doing. You want to find (and fix) your book's mistakes *before* launch, not after.

## What's in each chapter

I suggest reading this guide sequentially from start to finish. It's quite short and the concepts build on each other. But if you'd prefer to skip around, here's what's coming up:

- Chapter 2 — designing your book's foundations for long-lasting recommendability and organic growth
- Chapter 3 — using reader conversations to begin testing and improving your book before it has been written, saving future rewrites and verifying that you're on the right path
- Chapter 4 — improving your book's engagement, readability, and value-per-page through the lens of reader experience
- Chapter 5 — the practicalities of working with beta readers, including how to find, recruit, and manage them
- Chapter 6 — continuing with beta readers, we'll look at the most valuable feedback they can provide and how to use it to make a better book
- Chapter 7 — four reliable marketing options to find your first 1,000 readers and seed organic growth
- Chapter 8 — tactical tips for optimizing the sales, profitability, royalties, and growth of a finished title
- You'll also find an Interlude and Appendix addressing common questions about the tasks, timelines, and tools of writing and publishing a book

If you'd like to say hello, I'm rob@robfitz.com or @robfitz on Twitter. Additional resources, interviews, and our authors' community are at writeusefulbooks.com.

# Why I'm a relevant source of advice

Back in 2013, I wrote a short book called *The Mom Test* that taught entrepreneurs how to gather better customer feedback. In its first month, it earned a paltry $535. Eight years later, thanks to steady word of mouth, it has passed $12k in monthly royalties and continues to grow. It's now taught at universities like MIT, Harvard, and UCL; recommended by startup accelerators like YCombinator and Seedcamp; and used as a training manual at a wide range of businesses. It has hit #1 in most of its Amazon categories and has been translated by enthusiastic readers into nearly ten languages. All of this happened while I was largely ignoring the book and doing approximately zero active marketing.

I self-published, had no editor or professional help, and launched a book full of typos. And yet, despite its many flaws, the book has proven both profitable and long-lasting, earning more than $500k in total royalties thus far. The first six years' growth in monthly profits (up until $10k per month) is shown in the graph below. You'll notice that there was no big launch or magic bullet — just a steady, organic climb:

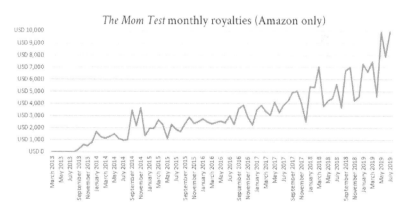

The Mom Test monthly royalties (Amazon only)

"Up and to the right" is an unusual shape for the sales of a book, with most nonfiction titles (including bestsellers) peaking within the first twelve weeks and then falling off a cliff:[1]

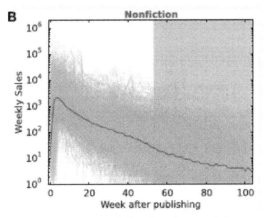

In 2019, I released my second book, *The Workshop Survival Guide* (coauthored with Devin Hunt), about designing and teaching educational workshops. While it's final success is still too early to call, it appears to be following a similar trajectory to The Mom Test, except better. Its sales at *month* five were the same as The Mom Test's at *year* five and it now generates a steady several thousand per month in royalties, again without any hands-on marketing. (I'll explain exactly how and why this works throughout the rest of this guide.)

Look inside ↓

**The Workshop Survival Guide: How to design and teach educational workshops that work every time**

Paperback – June 5, 2019

by Rob Fitzpatrick ˅ (Author), Devin Hunt ˅ (Author), & 1 more

★★★★½ ˅    172 ratings

Need to run a workshop? Your attendees are trusting you with their time and attention. What are you giving them in return?

As a small disclaimer, there are countless ways to write a great book and plenty of great authors who do the exact opposite of what I'm

---

[1] From the SpringerLink article *Success in books: a big data approach to bestsellers*: permanent.link/to/wub/springerbigdata.

about to advise. That's all fine. I'm not trying to create a grand unified theory of books or to say that anyone else's way is wrong. I just want to shine a light on a path that leads reliably toward creating nonfiction that is successful, impactful, and recommendable. And in the traditionally hit-driven, feast-or-famine world of books, there's something to be said for reliability.

## The goal of book marketing is to stop needing to do it

Books are inexpensive products. As such, investing loads of time into active, hands-on marketing is unlikely to sell enough copies per hour to return a meaningful income. The solution to this conundrum — and the whole premise of this guide — is to design something so useful that readers can't help but recommend it.

As such, I invest practically 100% of my effort into creating the most useful book possible — testing it with real readers at every step — and treat marketing as largely an afterthought. Not because marketing isn't important, but because marketing a useful book is the easiest thing in the world.

You'll still need to grind your way toward reaching the first several hundred readers yourself, which does involve some hands-on effort. Without that original seed audience, there would be nobody able to recommend your book and organic growth couldn't happen. But this initial "seed" marketing is a temporary task, requiring somewhere between a few weeks and a few months of part-time labor.

Once your book's audience has been seeded, you may optionally decide to continue hustling to accelerate its growth and impact. But if you would prefer to spend your time on other activities, then you'll be happy to hear that for properly designed nonfiction, ongoing marketing becomes an *option* rather than an *obligation*.

# The motivations and business models of nonfiction

Writing a useful book is too big of a project to be undertaken cynically. If you aren't clear on why you're getting into it, then you may have a tough time getting through the hard parts. I've asked quite a few authors why they were bothering, and here's what they told me.

Emotional motivations:

- Beginnings — to explore, plant a flag, and build a reputation in an interesting space where the author intends to remain
- Closure — to capture the lessons learned from some stage of life, allowing the author to move on
- Impact — to spread important knowledge beyond the author's direct reach
- Curiosity — to spend the time researching, wrestling with, and deeply understanding an irresistible topic
- Craft — they simply love the act of writing or teaching

Financial goals:

- Freedom via royalties — reliable, passive income to escape the rat race
- Increased earnings via reputation — a multiplier to speaking fees, consulting rates, and general career advancement
- Entrepreneurship via audience-building — using the book as one piece of a larger strategy around building an audience that can be cross-sold into additional products, services, or events

All three financial models are valid and profitable, depending on what you want. Although if you care primarily about freedom via royalties, then I'd strongly suggest self-publishing.

# Publishers, self-publishing, and profitability

This guide will apply equally well to both traditionally published and self-published titles. (I use both options for my books, depending on the country.) But if you haven't already sold your rights, the trade-offs are worth considering.

Self-publishing does require more work, but you'll earn 5x more royalties for life (50-70% instead of 8-15%) while also maintaining full control over your work and its future. To compensate for your reduced royalties, a publisher would need to sell at least 5x more copies than you could manage on your own. And in theory, they can.

Unfortunately (and understandably), publishers don't want to blow their marketing budget on an unproven book, so they prefer to "wait and see" until it has been de-risked, which typically means that you are either already a best-selling author (reputation), already possess an adoring audience waiting to buy your stuff (platform), or have already sold at least 10,000 copies of your book (momentum).

As an unproven author negotiating with a publisher, much of the discussion will revolve around how *you* are going to promote *your own* book, which isn't what most new authors expect. Until you're proven, it's more accurate to view a publisher as your book's investor, production assistant, and distributor rather than as its marketer.

There are many flavors of publishers, so it's hard to generalize. But you can get a sense of where you stand by looking at the combination of guaranteed marketing assistance alongside the cash advance. For big, traditional publishers, these two numbers are correlated. An advance of $50k+ suggests that they take your book quite seriously and are therefore also quite likely to support it with a guaranteed marketing spend. Whereas a lower advance (especially of $10k or less, which is typical for unproven and unplatformed authors) suggests that they're going to wait and see. Alternatively, some smaller indie publishers will compensate for lower advances by providing significantly more guaranteed marketing (or much higher royalties), which can also be a fine deal.

In any case, there's a trick to getting the best of both worlds. Savvy authors have recently been choosing to self-publish their first 10,000 copies and then transition afterwards into a publishing deal. If you're able to go this route, you'll receive full royalties from the first 10k sales (worth approximately $55k more than the royalties you'd receive from a publisher on that number of copies sold[2]) and can then enter contract negotiations from a position of strength since your book is already de-risked. This approach was used by Gabriel Weinberg and Justin Mares (authors of *Traction*) and by Alex Osterwalder and Yves Pigneur (authors of *Business Model Generation*), who each ended up getting *insane* deals for first-time authors. It's a strong hybrid model that maximizes early profits without sacrificing eventual scale.

## Start before you're ready

You don't need to have all the answers before getting started — your readers will help you find your way. E. L. Doctorow said it best:

> *Writing [a book] is like driving a car at night. You can see only as far as your headlights, but you can make the whole trip that way.*

As long as you know where you're trying to get to (Chapter 2) and are able to see the obstacles in front of you (via reader conversations and beta reading, Chapters 3 and 5-6), then you can find your way toward something wonderful.

Beyond that, allow me to share a few additional points of reassurance.

First, your early drafts are *supposed* to be terrible. Every first draft is a dumpster fire. That's okay. All writing begins by being awful and only starts to shine through rewrites, beta reading, and editing. A

---

[2] The $55k boost is due to earning average royalties of about $7 per book instead of $1.50 (a difference of $5.50 per copy) multiplied by the 10k copies that you would have had to hustle on your own in either case. The comparison isn't exactly apples-to-apples since self-publishing carries a bit more effort and expense, but even after adjusting for that, it's still a substantial difference.

draft is still a baby; it's unfair to judge it by the standards of a grown-up book.

Second, creating useful nonfiction is a task of manual labor, not genius. When people say they're "bad at writing," this usually just means that they're unwilling to spend sufficient time on feedback and editing. Yes, it may be slow. But being able to do something slowly is very different from being unable to do it at all.

Third, even if you were recently an amateur in your topic, fear not. By still remembering how it feels to stand in the shoes of a beginner, you'll write with an empathy and understanding that is impossible for the "natural expert" or "world's best" to match. That's a real edge.

Fourth, although writing a useful book does take time, you'll begin receiving feedback, support, and pre-orders from real readers long before the book is finished. And if you're anything like me, nothing will keep you as motivated as knowing that you're already helping real readers who are eagerly awaiting the next version.

Let's get started.

# CHAPTER 2

# Designing nonfiction for long-lasting recommendability

Authors tend to view reader recommendations as a bit of a happy accident. But you don't *hope* for recommendations; you *design* for them.

Consider the differences between two of my all-time favorite books about writing:

- ○ Paul Hendrickson's wonderful biography of Ernest Hemingway: *Hemingway's Boat: Everything He Loved in Life, and Lost*
- ○ Steven Pressfield's handbook: *The War of Art: Break Through the Blocks and Win Your Inner Creative Battles*

Both books wrestle artfully with the thorny question of how to fit the challenges of a creative life within the constraints of a real one. Each is masterful and authentic, and both maintain the same excellent rating of around 4.5 stars.

Yet I've found myself recommending the latter about fifty times more often than the former, and it appears I'm not alone. *Hemingway's Boat* currently has 250 reader reviews, while *The War of Art* has 10,000. That's a 40-to-1 difference in sales, royalties, and impact. From our perspective as authors, this imbalance in recommendability is the million dollar mystery, and unravelling it is our goal throughout this chapter.

## Useful books are problem-solving products

You can divide nonfiction books into two categories by their purpose to the reader:

1. Pleasure-givers ("interesting", "fascinating", "beautiful")
2. Problem-solvers ("useful", "actionable", "clarifying")

Pleasure-givers are crafted like art or literature, as a solitary act of genius. Whereas problem-solvers ought to be designed and built like products, through a reader-centric process of testing and refinement.

The word "problem" in "problem-solver" is being used somewhat loosely, and could include helping a reader to receive any sort of tangible outcome, such as to:

- Achieve a goal or undergo a process
- Answer a question or understand a concept
- Improve a skill or develop a toolkit
- Resolve a fear or inspire a change
- Adjust their perspective or improve their life

By shaping your book around this sort of clear promise and outcome, you fundamentally change its behavior in the marketplace.

To become a big hit, pleasure-givers typically rely on either PR momentum or a famous, well-platformed author. If everyone is talking about the latest biography of Steve Jobs (i.e., PR momentum), then everybody else starts to wonder what it's all about, which a savvy, well-positioned author can leverage to great success. Or if an already famous author releases a new book, long-time fans are quite likely to give it a try. This works out rather well for the fortunate few but is an unforgiving, winner-take-all environment for new authors.

Problem-solvers (i.e., useful books) behave differently. Their success is more meritocratic and within your control. Importantly, this category of books can be reliably designed, tested, and *proven* to be valuable to your readers, even prior to publication, which massively reduces the uncertainty and risk around creating something successful.

Confusingly, nearly all of the advice you've ever heard about "writing a book" is actually about writing a pleasure-giver, and is at best irrelevant and often harmful when applied to a problem-solver. So let's set aside that faulty intuition and start with what matters most: your book's promise to its reader.

## Make a clear promise and put it on the cover

Here's the secret to a five-star Amazon rating: be clear enough about what your book is promising that people can decide they don't need it. It may seem counterintuitive to try to drive potential readers away. But good books receive bad reviews after making too broad of a promise and luring the wrong people into buying. You can't fully prevent bad reviews from *ever* happening, but you can certainly make them a rare exception by plainly stating who your book is for and what they're going to get out of reading it.

Building your book around this sort of tangible outcome isn't as restrictive as it sounds. Beyond the obvious genres of how-tos and tutorials (called "prescriptive nonfiction"), nearly every style and topic of nonfiction can be designed as a problem-solver. For example, here are a few popular titles that fall outside of the traditional how-to:

- ○ *The Artist's Way: A Spiritual Path to Higher Creativity*, by Julia Cameron, helps readers reconnect with childlike creativity through a series of daily journaling exercises.
- ○ *The Dictator's Handbook: Why Bad Behavior is Almost Always Good Politics*, by Bruce Bueno de Mesquita and Alastair Smith, equips readers with a mental model for understanding why politicians make such seemingly bizarre decisions.

- *Quiet: The Power of Introverts in a World That Can't Stop Talking*, by Susan Cain, uses a combination of personal anecdotes and academic research to help introverts understand, appreciate, and leverage their natural strengths.
- *The Personal MBA: Master the Art of Business*, by Josh Kauffman, offers a concise summary and reference of all topics covered in a full MBA program.

Specificity is good. When I was learning to sail, I didn't buy an encyclopedic tome of everything to do with boats. Instead, I bought a handful of focused problem-solvers with titles like *Manoeuvring at Close Quarters Under Power* (Johnson), *Single-Handed Sailing* (Evans), and *Living on 12 Volts with Ample Power* (Smead and Ishihara). These books were valuable not in spite of their specificity, but because of it.

It's possible to reframe nearly any topic around a clear promise to the reader. For example, a collection of sixteenth-century essays by Michel de Montaigne is, for most readers, a source of "entertainment" in the form of humanized philosophy and history. But by repurposing that same source material around a clear value proposition, Sarah Bakewell created the wonderful philosophical problem-solver *How to Live: Or A Life of Montaigne in One Question and Twenty Attempts at an Answer*.

The husband and wife author team Will and Ariel Durant even applied this tactic to their own body of work. Having spent more than fifty years researching and writing their eleven-volume magnum opus, *The Story of Civilization*, they distilled it all down into a quick, 100-page problem-solver called *The Lessons of History*. Despite the latter requiring roughly a fiftieth of the time to write, its sales have outstripped those of all their other books combined. Why? Because it offered readers an *outcome* instead of just a story.

Your book's promise should appear in (or at least be strongly implied by) its title and/or subtitle. My all-time favorite nonfiction title is *How to Stay Alive in the Woods*, by Bradford Angier. Can you guess what that book is promising? Are you able to judge its relevance to your needs and goals? Do you know which of your friends might enjoy hearing about it? Absolutely. And as a result, it has sold 800k copies across twenty years despite competing against plenty of similar books that are arguably better. In my view, that's the direct result of making a clearer promise on its cover.

Still, it can sometimes be a bit tricky to find the right words to clearly and concisely describe your book's promise. The best way I've found to get there is to try it out in conversation. When someone asks what you're working on, attempt to describe the book in just one or two sentences. And then you need to do the hardest thing of all: to shut up and listen to them completely misinterpret and misunderstand what you're trying to do.

Each time you try describing it to someone, you'll get a little bit closer. And once people are immediately getting it — without requiring you to clarify or correct anything substantial — then you'll know you've found the words. Put them on your cover.

## Decide who it isn't for

A book's promise is meaningless until paired with a certain type of reader. My first book, *The Mom Test*, isn't anywhere close to the best book about sales or customer research — at least, not for everyone. But it absolutely *is* the best book about those topics for introverted technical entrepreneurs.

The same concept applies in all product design. Designing the world's best TV for *everyone* is impossible. How could you possibly hope to figure out the right price point or feature set? Whereas designing the world's best TV *for a specific type of someone* — the hearing impaired, parents of young kids, executive boardrooms — becomes instantly tractable.

Nearly every author attempts to include too much stuff for too many different types of readers. But that's a recipe for writing something mediocre for everybody and mind-blowing for nobody — every chapter that the amateur adores, the expert endures, and vice versa.

Here's how April Dunford described her choices while designing the enormously successful *Obviously Awesome: How to Nail Product Positioning so Customers Get It, Buy It, Love It*:

> *Most business books are "idea books." They don't give you one little word about how to get it done. My book was going to be the book about how to actually do it.*
>
> *The publishers said, "Hmm, that doesn't sound like it's going to sell a lot of copies. How many people do positioning?" And I said, "Lots of people! The CEO of every startup. Marketing people. Product people. Lots of them!"*
>
> *And then [the publishers] would always want me to write a different book. They'd say, "Oooo, why don't you write a book on how to position your life — then we could sell one to everybody!" But that is a book I have zero interest in writing and that's not what I'm trying to do here. I'm trying to write the book that helps you get something done.*[3]

The above anecdote is not intended as a dig at idea books — the right idea at the right moment can be enormously useful. The point is that, in order to make something valuable for *somebody*, you must be willing to define and defend what your book isn't.

You can probably guess what Dunford did next: she ignored the advice to target everybody, created something dense with practical value for a very specific type of reader, unlocked remarkable organic growth, and saw her already-successful consulting business quadruple within the next two years.

Throughout the writing process, you'll receive a bucketload of well-intentioned criticism, advice, and suggestions from all sorts of people. Before allowing those comments to take hold of your soul, take a moment to reflect on who your book is really for. If you're writing for beginners, should you worry that an expert finds it all a

---

[3] Watch my full interview with April Dunford: writeusefulbooks.com/dunford/

bit elementary? Or if writing for experts, should you worry that the beginner is confused? Probably not.

The reason this matters is that nobody recommends the second-best solution. So you need to become the best. Not for everyone, but for someone. And the easiest way to manage that is by speaking directly to their situation and context by excluding everybody else. Far better to be loved by someone than ignored by everyone.

## Weak scope / strong scope

Your book is under no obligation to start from the beginning, to serve everybody, or to cover everything. Pick the piece you're best at, for the people you care most deeply about serving, at the moment in their journey where you can really help them, and forget about everything else. These crucial decisions will define your book's scope.

The scope of a useful book is like the executive summary of a new business. It's an as-brief-as-possible description of what it is, who it's for, and why they'll pay for it:

*Scope = Promise + Reader profile + Who it's not for + What it won't cover*

*(And we'll soon add recommendability and longevity as the final two considerations of a strong scope.)*

*The Mom Test began* its life with an extremely weak scope. I was aware of the book's core value, but had diluted that useful core by trying to do too many jobs for too many different types of readers.

My original, bad scope was:

Everyone interested in business should read this book. *(Overly broad and doomed to mediocrity.)*

If you don't know anything about startups, I'll explain how they work. And if you don't know about Customer

Development, I'll explain that, too. And I'll then convince you why talking to customers is worth the effort. *(Oof, a lot of super boring theory for readers who already understand this stuff.)*

And once you believe *all that,* I'll teach you how to do it properly. *(A-ha! We've finally reached the real value. Assuming any readers have stuck around this long.)*

Wow, that was awful. How could I have thought that would ever be a compelling product? That scope describes a book with low value-per-page that's guaranteed to flounder and fail.

I didn't fix the scope by figuring out what to *add* (or how to write it more beautifully), but by figuring out what to *delete.* The path became clear after asking one crucial question:

*What does my ideal reader already know and believe?*

I soon decided that if people didn't already understand and believe in the value of Customer Development (i.e., one of the theoretical foundations that my advice was built on), then my book simply wasn't for them. This allowed me to cut all the early theory and justification and begin with what I actually wanted to say, which was about how to do it.

The revised scope sounded like this:

*If you're a tech entrepreneur struggling to run useful customer interviews, this book will help you understand why the conversations are going wrong and how to run them properly.*

That's sharper. That told me who the book was for, which tone to take, what to include, and what to leave out. It allowed me to start with a bang, delivering real value from the first page of the first chapter.

Your book's scope should also be guided by your own goals and interests as its author. An important moment for *The Workshop Survival Guide* was deciding that our ideal readers would already have a workshop to teach, and that we could therefore skip all discussion of selling tickets, negotiating with clients, building a reputation, and the rest of the "business" side of workshops. Would some readers have enjoyed those topics? Definitely. But since we weren't excited about writing them, and since the book still offered a desirable outcome without them, we simply called those topics out of scope.

Three helpful lines of questioning to strengthen your scope:

1.  When someone decides to buy and read your book, what are they trying to achieve or accomplish with it? Why are they bothering? After finishing it, what's different in their life, work, or worldview? That's your book's promise.
2.  What does your ideal reader already know and believe? If they already believe in the importance of your topic, then you can skip (or hugely reduce) the sections attempting to convince them of its worth. Or if they already know the basics, then you can skip those.
3.  Who is your book *not* for and what is it *not* doing? If you aren't clear on who you're leaving out, then you'll end up writing yourself into rabbit holes, wasting time on narrow topics that only a small subset of your readers actually care about. Deciding who it isn't for will allow you to clip those tangential branches.

Your scope will still evolve and improve as you proceed through the process, so it doesn't need to be perfect. But it's worth documenting your current best guesses — you'll soon begin gaining real reader data, and having a hypothesis in hand will help you make the most of it.

Of course, on its own, a brilliant scope is not enough. Your book's contents also need to work.

## DEEP books vs. ineffective problem-solvers

For a problem-solver to be recommended frequently enough to endure and grow, it requires four qualities, represented with the acronym DEEP:[4]

1. Desirable — readers want what it is promising (Chapters 2 and 3)
2. Effective — it delivers real results for the average reader (Chapters 3 and 5-6)
3. Engaging — it's front-loaded with value, has high value-per-page, and feels rewarding to read (Chapter 4)
4. Polished — it is professionally written and presented (Chapter 6 and the Appendix)

Of the four requirements of DEEP, the earlier requirements dominate the later ones. If nobody wants it or it doesn't work (requirements #1 and #2), then it doesn't matter how engaging or well-written it is (requirements #3 and #4). And the second requirement — Effectiveness — is where nonfiction most commonly misses the mark.

Imagine buying a can opener for $12.99, getting it home, spending three hours with it, and still being unable to open a can. You would be justifiably irate.

The can opener would be a product with a desirable promise ("I want to open a can"), but which failed to follow through with an effective solution ("But I still can't"). And while this is thankfully rare in the realm of kitchen appliances, it's dishearteningly common in nonfiction.

---

[4] I'm always a bit suspicious of too-clever acronyms, as if the author started with the acronym and then worked backwards to fill it out. If you feel similarly, then you'll be pleased to hear that this acronym was originally the far less clever "DERP," with "Readable/Rewarding" as the third requirement. But my editor Adam refused to let me put that into print, and I soon found "Engaging" as a more informative synonym. If you ever find me in a cafe and recommend a book as being mega derpy, I'll know that you're giving it the highest praise.

The fatal flaw of ineffective books isn't the writing. They're generally well-written, well-edited, well-proofed, and well-styled. But they don't *work*. Six months later, if you ask a reader what they're doing differently because of the book, you'll see that it failed to make even a drop of difference in their lives. Ineffective books can still have a "successful" launch (normally when fueled by a large author platform or heavy marketing/PR), but they don't last. Reading one is like buying a brilliantly packaged sandwich only to discover that there's no filling between the bread.

In the world of education, there's a phenomenon called "pseudoteaching." From the perspective of a classroom observer, pseudoteaching appears flawless: the lesson and its delivery are clear, simple, energetic, and coherent. But for whatever reason, students fail to actually learn. Pseudoteaching mimics the *appearance* of brilliant teaching without sharing its impact. The knowledge fails to cross the air gap. Once you start measuring the student's actual results (the outcome) instead of the teacher's performance (the input), you'll find that a polished and energetic delivery is worthless unless the teacher has first spent the time ensuring that the underlying lesson *works*.

Much nonfiction falls into the same trap, and our shelves now overflow with beautifully written page-turners that don't work. The intended knowledge somehow fails to cross the air gap from either author-to-book or from book-to-reader.

In fact, it's so rare for a book to deliver on its promise that readers will adore you for doing just that one thing. I've heard plenty of people recommend a messy-but-effective book by saying:

> *Listen, it's terribly written and full of typos and has a cover that appears to have been drawn by a distracted toddler, but it's got something inside that's just too important to miss. It's going to change your life. You've got to read it. Trust me.*

But I've never heard even a single person recommend a problem-solver with the inverse argument of:

> *This book is a real zero-impact way to spend thirteen dollars and three hours. But you can tell that the author is super smart, the cover is gorgeous, and there's not even a single typo. You're going to love it.*

This is why the typical approach to book creation is backwards: the misguided author begins by writing, rewriting, and editing a full manuscript, and only then starts figuring out whether readers want it and whether it works. But by that point, it's too late to fix big issues without redoing absolutely everything.

You ideally want to nail all four requirements of DEEP. But unless you get the first two right, then even the most artful prose (or the cleverest marketing) won't have a chance to matter.

## Word of mouth can be anticipated and designed for

With these foundational ideas in place — solving a problem, making a promise, targeting a specific type of reader, and ensuring that the knowledge works — we're finally ready to untangle the mystery of recommendability.

Here's how a new reader typically finds out about *The Mom Test*:

> *A new entrepreneur is starting a business. Everyone is telling them to "go talk to their customers." So they try, but it's harder than it sounds. Maybe the conversations are awkward, the feedback is unreliable, or they can't even find anyone to talk to.*

> *During their next meeting with an advisor or peer, they mention how tough it has been. And the other person says, "Oh, I know the solution to your problem. It's this book called The Mom Test."*

*(Alternatively, they type their problem into Google and find an article written by another entrepreneur saying essentially the same thing.)*

This narrative represents a sort of "recommendation loop" that gets triggered by someone complaining about (or seeking a solution to) a high-priority "problem." If that happens frequently enough, then the book's growth becomes self-sustaining.

You can — and should — write out this sort of recommendation story for your own book idea. It puts you in the perspective of your readers when they are first seeking (or hearing about) your book and helps you better empathize with their situation, goals, and context in that moment.

And then, once it's written down, attempt to make it stronger. Ask yourself:

1.  Is your book's promise Desirable enough that people will readily complain about, receive advice, give advice, and search for solutions to it? When someone encounters this problem/question/goal, is finding a solution a top priority or simply a nice-to-have?
2.  If your book could have several possible promises, does one have more "hair on fire" urgency for a certain type of reader?
3.  Of your several potential reader profiles, does one more actively search for (or give) advice and recommendations? Do any feel the pain more sharply? If so, they'll fuel a stronger, faster recommendation loop.

This is the first of several moments when you can go back to strengthen your scope. A book's organic growth will live or die based on its recommendation loop. If your current scope doesn't lend itself to strong recommendability, then consider adjusting it until it does. (Of course, your book also needs to be Effective enough to be recommended as the solution, which we'll return to.)

The recommendation loop for *The Workshop Survival Guide* is triggered by the stressful preparation before an important workshop or presentation. The cost of failure is high and the event's date can't be moved, which makes it an urgent, must-solve priority. At some point during those tense days or weeks, the soon-to-be-facilitator mentions their stress to a friend or colleague (triggering the loop) and gets pointed toward the book as the best available solution (fulfilling the loop).

Afterwards — having received the value and used it to deliver a brilliant workshop — they'll become able to recommend the book to others, creating a virtuous cycle of organic evangelism that looks like this:

⭐⭐⭐⭐⭐ **Hands Down THE BEST Material on Designing and Running Effective Workshop**
Reviewed in the United States on January 19, 2020
Verified Purchase

Got this book on recommendation the weekend before I was to deliver two workshops. Turned a terrifying, stressful preparation process into an absolute breeze. This book is short enough to be carried around for quick reference but detailed enough to really answer all the important questions of facilitation. I am now a workshop-giving machine!

You can probably now see why I've found myself recommending *The War of Art* so much more frequently than *Hemingway's Boat*, despite loving both equally. It's because the former (1) convincingly solves (2) a painful problem (3) for a certain type of reader (4) who often mentions it to me. At which point, how could I *not* recommend it? In other words, despite being broadly "about" the same topic, *The War of Art* has a recommendation loop, and *Hemingway's Boat* doesn't.

A recommendation loop will function even if people don't know that they're looking for a book. For example, after moving to a new city, someone might confide to a friend, "It's been hard meeting people, and I guess I'm feeling a little bit lonely." And they are told, in reply, "Oh, you have to read this book — it helped me out so much. It's called X."

## Recommendability creates a mini-monopoly and pricing power

Traditionally, books are a commodity product with low differentiation, which is why they all share approximately the same cover price. But if someone has been personally told that your book is *the* solution to the problem currently ruining their life, how likely are they to end up buying a different book? In most cases, they won't even think about it and will just buy yours.

Which means that *recommendability removes competition.* This has considerable implications for marketing, pricing, and profits.

In theory, *The Mom Test* has plenty of competitors. There's even a strikingly similar book written by someone far more famous and credible than myself, which the author gives away for free to bring in consulting clients. If a new reader were to stumble across our two books side by side without a recommendation, it's essentially a roll of the dice to determine which they'll end up picking (if they even buy one at all). But if my book has been personally recommended? That's complete immunity to all competitive dynamics.

This is why I was happy to launch *The Mom Test* at the relatively high price of $30 for such a short book, despite having no personal reputation or platform at the time. I figured that if people were hearing about the book via individual recommendations, then I could price it however I liked. (See Chapter 8 for a few more notes on optimizing pricing.)

Most books drown in a sea of undifferentiated competition. Recommendability offers a boat and a moat. Of course, for recommendability to deliver maximum benefit, you book must be built to last.

## Write for the back catalog with timeless content

A useful book's organic growth will accelerate over time as more people receive enough value to become able to recommend it. As such, you gain compounding benefits by writing something that will remain relevant for many years.

*The Mom Test* required three years' growth to regularly exceed $3k in monthly royalties. Now that the book has found its legs, the royalties from its most recent two years have surpassed those from its first six. Imagine if I had written it in such a way that it lost relevance after only a handful of years... I may as well not have bothered.

Selling 50,000 books in a twelve-week launch window is *hard*, requiring an enchanted cocktail of luck, skill, resources, and hustle. But if your book is able to endure for ten years, you could hit that same lofty milestone (worth about $350k in total royalties if self-published) by selling 100 copies per week. A hundred copies per week isn't trivial, but it's doable.

For a traditionally designed book, time is the great enemy. But for something long-lasting and useful, the passage of time is an incredible ally that will lift your book far higher than you could ever achieve on your own.

The industry term for these enduring titles is "back catalog." They're the books that defy the odds, remaining relevant and recommended for years. And entering the back catalog is *ridiculously* profitable. According to author and entrepreneur Seth Godin, back catalog books are responsible for 90% of the publishing industry's profits while requiring only 2% of its marketing budget.[5] As such, it's worth intentionally designing your book to get there.

Beyond creating something DEEP[6] and useful, you must obey two additional requirements for your book to enter the back catalog:

1. Pick a promise that will remain relevant and important for 5+ years
2. Avoid overreliance on temporary tools, trends, and tactics that are likely to become quickly dated

---

[5] From Seth's blog: permanent.link/to/wub/backlist

[6] As a reminder, DEEP = Desirable promise, Effective knowledge and advice, Engaging reader experience, Polished and professional presentation

*The Mom Test* is now established in the back catalog, which is lovely. The book's promise is inherently timeless (i.e., understanding what customers care about), so I got the first piece for free. The bigger design decision was about staying clear of trends. At the time I wrote it, customer conversations were closely tied to the then-buzzing world of Lean Startup. By choosing to discuss the enduring foundations while staying mostly clear of the temporary trend, I ended up writing something that will (hopefully) continue to be valuable.

In *The Workshop Survival Guide*, Devin and I were hugely tempted to include a tutorial on designing custom themes for slide decks — a topic that was relevant, useful, and frequently requested by beta readers. But we finally decided against it, since it would have "dated" us to the 2019 versions of slide software. (Although these sorts of additional, timely resources are a perfect fit for your website, where they act as both a marketing tool for gaining new readers, a reason for existing readers to visit and offer you their email, and/or a potential upsell. More on that in Chapters 7 and 8.)

To see why this all matters, consider *The 4-Hour Workweek* (2007), by Tim Ferriss, a category-breaking bestseller that soothed a painful emotional "problem" around disillusionment with the 9-to-5. The book enjoyed incredible success due to both its own strengths plus Ferriss's incomparable skill and hustle as a marketer. And yet, rereading it now, a dozen years later, a significant percentage of its content feels — at least to me — irrelevant and dated. Of course, huge amounts of value still exist! The good stuff is just hidden between extended discussions of tools and tactics that haven't aged quite so well. And when only a portion of the book remains relevant, the whole is diminished.

That's not to say you can't make *any* mention of stuff that dates. In the 1996 edition of Andy Grove's otherwise timeless *Only the Paranoid Survive* (a classic problem-solver about management and corporate strategy), there's one now-anachronistic section about the hidden potential of some up-and-coming thing called "the internet." But that one section is easily forgiven when nestled within a book that is otherwise as relevant today as it was twenty-five years ago.

Plus, sometimes, as an author, you'll *really need* to mention a particular tool or technology, and being overzealous about avoiding these references can make a book feel frustratingly abstract. Overall, the bits that date should be brief, infrequent, valuable for today's readers, and easy for tomorrow's to skip.

If you're writing about a fast-changing topic like computer programming or regional tax law, then there's no way to avoid tying yourself to today's minutia. If that's the case, then you can compensate by regularly releasing updated editions. That's a bit of a chore, but it's also a competitive advantage when done well.

To create a book that lasts and grows, the formula is simple: do the best job of solving an important problem for a reader who cares, without anchoring yourself to temporary tools, tactics, or trends. That's partly about good scoping and partly about writing something that delivers real results to the average reader. And to accomplish that second goal, you'll want to begin testing the book's foundations with real people, even before it has even been written.

# CHAPTER 3

# Improve your book before you've written it

Imagine a friend who is designing and building a new house for their family. But instead of gathering feedback on the early designs from the people who will be living there, they just start piling up bricks.

Months later, they're finally proud enough of the work-in-progress to reveal it to the rest of the family, who gently suggest that it might be nice to have another bedroom. Or perhaps for the whole thing to be placed slightly higher up the hill? The well-intentioned builder says, "Hmm, great suggestions," and begins tearing down and rearranging everything. It takes ages. After a couple iterations, they're out of time and out of energy, so they call it good enough. They say, "Well, I wish I could have done a little bit more, but honestly, building a house is just such hard work — every little adjustment takes months!"

As absurd as it sounds, that's exactly what most authors do with books. They write in secret, piling up a manuscript's worth of beautiful words and only *then* start figuring out whether people want it and it works. But by that point, even small changes have become unnecessarily complex and costly, leading to wasted time, extra rewrites, and a final product that falls far short of its full potential.

# Listening and teaching are part of writing

A guiding principle of product design is that the more iterations you can do — while in front of real users — the better the product will become. The same applies to designing a useful book. But rewriting an entire manuscript requires so much time that there's typically an upper limit on how many iterations are possible. The solution, as silly as it sounds, is to talk to people.

Done properly, these "reader conversations" will allow you to test and iterate on your book's underlying scope and structure without worrying about its *words*, and without needing to rewrite anything larger than a table of contents. This massively accelerates the speed of early iterations and allows you to construct your early drafts atop rock-solid foundations.

Depending on what you're trying to learn, you'll use two main styles of reader conversations:

1.  Listening/understanding conversations — to verify and improve your scope and rekindle reader empathy
2.  Teaching/helping conversations — to refine your table of contents and iterate on the book's underlying education design and structure

In practice, these two styles of conversations tend to overlap and blur together, so you needn't be overly strict about facilitation. For example, a "teaching conversation" might end up feeling more like a loose Q&A than a structured coaching session — that's fine.

Just be aware that *neither* of these conversations are about asking for opinions about your book idea ("So what do you think?"). Asking for opinions is just fishing for compliments.

The most impactful reader conversations happen early in the process, while you're still figuring out the scope and ToC and are free to make big, sweeping changes without rewriting anything. After that, it's a matter of personal preference whether you'd like to continue having a few conversations per week (I still do them). But the benefits from the earliest conversations are profound.

# Escape the curse of knowledge by listening to their life

Have you ever read a book (or listened to a lecture) by someone with so much expertise that they ended up becoming unintelligible to the novice? That's the curse of knowledge, and it kills an awful lot of books.

Books about chess, for example, are notoriously vulnerable to the curse of knowledge. Reading them tends to feel like receiving the unhelpful advice to "just be smarter." But one title that stands apart — and has remained a top-twenty chess bestseller for the past twenty years — is *The Amateur's Mind*, by Jeremy Silman. From Silman's Introduction to the book:

> *I often wondered what would happen if a teacher could really get inside the student's head. To accomplish this, I played games with my students, had them talk out loud before they made a move and after I made mine, and wrote down their thoughts. To my amazement, I was soon seeing problems that I never imagined they possessed.*

That last line is remarkable because Silman was far from inexperienced — he was already an International Master who had coached countless students and written a bestselling chess book. And yet, he still missed his readers' actual challenges until he stopped pitching his advice and started listening to their reality by having them literally narrate their own thoughts.

As the author, you'll typically be more experienced than your readers. To write something useful, you'll need to get back inside their heads and see the topic from their perspective. This sort of "reader empathy" allows you to escape the curse of knowledge as well as to anticipate common questions, objections, concerns, and confusions. It will help you to strike the right tone, tempo, and level of detail, and will make your early drafts ineffably *better*.

Plus, you'll be able to see which types of readers care most deeply about which issues (i.e., finding a Desirable scope), and these friendly first contacts will often develop into your earliest beta readers, testimonials, and evangelists. That's a lot of benefit from a few quick chats.

Unless your topic demands it, you probably won't need to be as structured as Silman. In most cases, a good listening conversation is just a friendly exploration of the reader's experiences, worldview, and decision-making:

> You've been dealing with X recently, right? Would you mind talking me through what you did and how it went? How did you decide to do it that way? What else did you try? What did you give up on or find unhelpful? Where did you search for help or guidance? What were the most frustrating moments? How did you eventually get over them? Did you read any books or blogs about it? Why (or why not)? Which ones were helpful and which were a waste? Why? What's still worrying or blocking you? Are you doing anything about it, or is it not that big of a deal?

This line of questioning leads to all manner of insights that will directly strengthen your scope and recommendation loop.

If you'd like, you can be even more casual than the above. For example, my listening conversations for this guide were set in motion by a very simple sort of prompt:

> Oh, you're writing a book? Amazing! How are you approaching it?

Or:

> You said you've always wanted to write a book — what's getting in your way?

The resulting conversations would open a window onto my readers' worldviews, perspectives, and current behaviors, revealing how they saw the issue and how I might be able to help them.

For *The Workshop Survival Guide*, Devin and I asked people where they were getting most stressed or stuck while preparing their workshops. We asked which parts were hardest, and where they felt that they were wasting the most time. We asked if anything had gone wrong at their previous workshop, and if anything was scaring them about the next one. And then we tried our best to write the book in a way that would speak to their context, soothe their fears, and solve their problems. Without this sort of baseline understanding, you're throwing darts in the dark.

Just remember that these sorts of conversations are *not* about pitching (or even describing) your book idea. In the context of building reader empathy, pitching will prevent deeper learning by both exposing your ego (which discourages negative feedback) as well as by suggesting that you've already figured out the details (which discourages big-picture feedback). You want insights into their life, not opinions about your idea.[7]

Once you begin to feel that your book's scope is resonating with your future readers, it's time to shift toward testing the Effectiveness of what it will contain. Which begins by writing down a first guess at a detailed table of contents.

## Fill your ToC with takeaways, not clickbait

Your ToC is the blueprint of your book's education design. To serve its purpose as a tool for design and feedback, it must be built from:

1. Clear, descriptive language
2. Detailed subsections.

I know that sounds self-evident, but nearly everybody gets it wrong.

---

[7] If you'd like significantly more detail about these sorts of listening conversations, grab a copy of *The Mom Test: How to talk to customers and learn if your business is a good idea when everyone is lying to you* (momtestbook.com).

For example, I was once helping a buddy with his education design, and he had a title that just said:

*Sales 101*

Okay, so that section is going to cover something foundational... But what is it actually saying? What is its learning outcome or takeaway? What does the reader gain from reading it? Upon being pushed a little bit, he clarified his real point:

*Good sales is about asking good questions*

Much better — that actually describes the top takeaway, so it should be the title.

But what if that section contained multiple major learning outcomes? In that case, we would leave the top-level title as a larger category, and add additional subsections with its specific takeaways.

Here's a ToC excerpt from *The Workshop Survival Guide*. Note that in most cases, the sections aren't only a vague "topic," but actually contain the primary learning outcome or takeaway:

| | |
|---|---|
| **Maintain goodwill with regular "a-ha" moments** | 6 |
| **Don't start with the slides (do start with the Skeleton)** | 8 |
| You need to know who's in the room | 9 |
| Add the coffee breaks before designing the content | 12 |
| Sharpen your Learning Outcomes | 15 |
| Each Learning Outcome is a cluster of related ideas | 18 |
| Workshop Outline + Schedule Chunks = Workshop Skeleton | 20 |
| **Vary the Teaching Formats to improve energy, attention, and learning** | 25 |
| **The five essential Teaching Formats** | 28 |
| Format 1: Lectures have their place | 29 |

This over-the-top descriptiveness is enormously helpful while testing and refining the book's structure and contents, since it allows you to visualize exactly what (and when) a reader is learning.

As a counter-example, although I absolutely adore Dave Canterbury's excellent *Bushcraft* series, I feel that he missed an opportunity to provide more informative titles, as in this ToC excerpt from the second book in his four-volume box set about wilderness survival:

Despite being well-organized and clean, a list of trees isn't exactly an information-rich mind-blower. This forces me, as a reader, to page through each and every section before discovering what they're actually about. That's a moderately irritating speed bump while sitting in my living room, but becomes dangerously unhelpful if I'm attempting to use it as an actual "field guide" during an exigent wilderness emergency.

As an avid reader of Canterbury's books, I'd much prefer if he had put the takeaways in the section titles, like this:

- Pine for fire-starting, food, and bandaging injuries
- Willow for carving, weaving, finding water, and as a pain-killer
- Poplar for carving, kindling, containers, and treating infections or itches
- Oak for construction, crafting, coal-fires, and medicine

Many authors appear to resist this level of detail due to a fear of inconsistency. Some sections (and many chapters) will defy clean summarization. Regardless, I feel that informative titles are valuable enough to be worth aiming for, even at the cost of consistency. Use them when possible. And when not possible, just fall back onto being as descriptive as you are able (and adding extra subsections if needed).

You can adjust the aesthetics and style of your titles later, once the book's structure has been tested and proven, toward the second half of beta reading. If you prefer long chapters without subsections, or if you want to use clever and punny titles, then that's the time to make the switch. But throughout the design and writing process, treat your ToC as what it really is: a detailed blueprint of your book's education design, learning outcomes, and takeaways.

## Teach the book to test its contents

Even the greatest standup comedians still test their fresh material in tiny basement bars, ready to face the confused silence of an unamused crowd. Because every good comedian knows that the first version of a new joke is a guess, not a guarantee. Before each of his fifteen HBO comedy specials, George Carlin would spend an entire year, in front of real audiences, distilling his new ideas down into a single hour of refined brilliance.

You'll want to follow more or less the same approach, which you can accomplish by "becoming the book" and teaching its contents to your future readers. By helping them through the process yourself, you'll learn what they need, and in what order. You'll figure out which examples resonate and which exercises work. All of which will end up directly improving both your ToC and your soon-to-be-written manuscript.

Due to how much *stuff* goes into a book, you probably won't be able to teach the whole thing in any single conversation. Instead, isolate one or two chapters that offer a desirable outcome for the particular person you are chatting with. Sit down and attempt to teach that slice of the ToC to them. Don't just describe what it will contain — help them to actually receive its value and achieve its promise. (Alternatively, you might prefer to run it as more of a Q&A or coaching conversation, where they share any questions and challenges, and you do your best to guide them through whatever comes up.)

Take good notes about what's working and what isn't. Whenever you're forced to improvise, repeat, or rephrase, treat it as an opportunity to iterate and improve your ToC.

Asking potential readers for these sorts of conversations is fairly straightforward. After all, you're basically just volunteering to give them free, expert guidance about an outcome that they care about:

*Hey, I remember that you were thinking about doing X a while back. Is that still on your mind? If so, I'd love to grab some time, answer any questions, and help you think through how to approach it.*

*The reason I bring this up is that I'm starting to work on a new book about the topic, and helping you through it would be super useful for me as research. And hopefully I can be helpful in return.*

*(Or for a more "professional" version, phrase it as an offer of free coaching/consulting in exchange for a follow-up call in a few weeks to hear how it ended up working for them.)*

You'll sometimes be lucky enough to find a potential reader who cares so deeply about your book's outcome that they will be willing (and delighted!) to spend considerable amounts of time with you. While writing *The Workshop Survival Guide*, Devin and I each "adopted" one aspiring facilitator, spending somewhere between twenty and forty hours with each throughout the book's creation. This allowed us to test the book's full process with them, see where they got stuck, and to identify the ideas that had sounded good in theory but failed in practice.

Incidentally, teaching conversations can also cure imposter syndrome. Instead of attempting to *believe* that your advice is worth sharing, go out and *prove* that it is by helping real people and seeing if it works. For example, the two facilitators that we coached in the anecdote above each saw their daily teaching fees quadruple while working with us (from around £500 to £2,000 per day), which went a long way toward convincing Devin and I that we were writing something worth the ink.

Writing is teaching, but harder. If a live session gets off track, you can notice the confusion and improvise your way through it; not so with a finished book. Which means that you need to test and solidify your educational design *in advance*.

You don't need to get it completely perfect just yet, because you'll still receive massive insight from beta reading (see Chapters 5 and 6). But if possible, it's best to catch the biggest issues at this early stage, while fixing them only costs an afternoon.

## How to find people to talk to

Here's the crucial insight about finding reader conversations: you don't need that many. Plus, you don't need them all at once — a few at the start and one or two per week throughout a book's creation is more than enough. This means that you don't require any sort of repeatable, scalable strategy. Instead, you can simply position yourself to benefit from a little bit of serendipity.

Begin with friendly first contacts. Given that you're deep enough into this topic to be writing a book about it, you probably already know a few relevant people who won't require any sort of clever justification to get chatting. Prioritize the ones who match the experience-level of your ideal readers.[8]

Second, plant a flag online. The simplest version — if your profession allows for it — is to add a link or blurb to your email signature explaining what you're doing with your book and how people can help. This will likely create only a small trickle of potential readers, but for now, a trickle is all you need.

Third, when people ask what you've been up to, start mentioning the book as "your thing." Some non-zero percentage will become animated with excitement ("Oh my gosh, you're writing a book about that!"), and when this happens, you've got an easy conversation on your hands. Avoid the temptation to schedule the

---

[8] Friendly first contacts will obviously be more biased (in a supportive way), but that only matters if you fall into the trap of pitching your idea and asking for opinions. As long as you steer the conversation away from your idea and keep it focused on either listening/understanding or teaching/helping, their potential bias won't matter.

chat for later — you're already talking to them, so just start learning what you want to learn.

Fourth and finally, if you'd prefer a more scalable approach, you can begin your pre-launch seed marketing (especially content marketing — see Chapter 7) while inviting superfans to opt in for reader conversations and beta reading. This does require investing more time, but it has the benefit of reaching beyond your own personal network (and doubling as the start of your seed marketing).

Unless you've got zero other options, don't waste time on direct cold outreach. People are busy and will almost never accept an invitation from a stranger to be interviewed (or review a manuscript).

Instead of trying to convince strangers to do something they don't want to do, spend your time finding the people who already care. And if *nobody* cares, their disinterest also means something.

## What if nobody wants to talk to you?

If you can't find a single person who is excited to chat about your topic, then it could mean that either:

1.  Your readers don't care about the book's promise (return to scoping until they do, adjusting either the reader or the promise)
2.  You don't know — or can't find — even a single potential reader (start dealing with that today)
3.  You don't actually care enough about this topic or reader to fuss with testing and refining a useful book (return to scoping until *you* care)

All three issues are book-killers if ignored, but can be easily resolved once you're aware of what's happening.

The first problem — a lukewarm reader — is evidence of an undesirable scope. Adjust either your promise or reader profile until you've found something that excites and motivates them.

The second — being unable to find even one potential reader — presents a more subtle danger, because it's generally an excuse instead of a truth. Authors rationalize it by believing that once their book is sufficiently fleshed out, readers will magically erupt from the woodwork to enjoy and evangelize it. But if you can't find even one reader now, then you're unlikely to find thousands of them later.

Most folks who claim not to know a single potential reader are actually just too nervous to ask for help. And that nervousness comes from believing they need to show a perfect, polished product.

But if you shift the conversation to be about your readers' lives instead of your ideas, then the initial invitation is as easy as saying:

> *Hey, I'm planning out a book about setting up an apartment veggie garden. I remember you once mentioned doing something like that before — would you mind talking me through what you tried and how it went? It would help me out so much and should only take about fifteen minutes. But I know everyone is super busy these days, so of course no worries if it's not a good time.*

If you really, truly can't reach a single potential reader, then you'll want to start dealing with that *today* instead of on launch day.

The third issue — you just can't be bothered — is more existential. If you're already feeling bored and disinterested by the prospect of talking to your readers at this early juncture, then you'll likely also skimp on all the other reader-centric activities that lead to a useful, long-lasting, recommendable book. That doesn't mean you should give up altogether, but it does suggest that you might want to adjust either topic or audience until you feel excited to engage with them.

Hiding from your readers is a slippery slope that causes a series of harmful decisions and consequences: skipping reader conversations, skipping beta reading, and launching without testimonials, reviews, or a seed audience. The more you're scared by the idea of talking to your readers, the more important it is to deal with now.

Because next up, you're writing a manuscript.

# Expand the tested ToC into a first draft

Having verified that people want it and it works (i.e., that your book is Desirable and Effective, the first two requirements of DEEP), it's time to write a first draft.

You don't need to draft the entire book, but should write enough to deliver the first big piece of value, allowing you to begin beta reading on that piece. Depending on your book's contents and structure, that might require one chapter, several chapters, or the whole thing. (And if you'd prefer to write the whole book regardless, that's fine too.)

If you're already happy putting words to paper, feel free to skip this Interlude and leap ahead to Chapter 4, which is about revising the first draft into an engaging reader experience. But if the idea of finding the time, doing the work, and wrangling the words gives you pause, then read on.

## The first draft is supposed to be a mess

For the first draft, most folks suggest just closing your eyes and getting it down.

As a way to outwit the internal critic, Hemingway quipped that you ought to "write drunk, edit sober." My editor, Adam, describes it as, "vomiting words onto the page." The main idea is to avoid slowing yourself down by rereading, self-judging, or fretting over what you've written.

You'll begin to reread, evaluate, and improve it during the second and third drafts. But for now, just get it down on paper.

Don't fix typos. Don't rework paragraphs to be more beautiful. Just follow the ToC that you've already verified via reader conversations. You'll still have a chance to make it pretty (or at least a bit less ugly) before exposing it to beta readers. The first draft is just to help you think.

Don't worry about front matter (introduction, foreword, etc.) or back matter (appendix, resources, etc.). Focus on the core content. The introduction will typically be the last thing you write, after understanding exactly what the book has matured into.

## Use your comfort tools to find your natural tone

Use whichever writing tools you're most comfortable with, even if that means pen and paper. You'll probably import the manuscript into a different tool for beta reading, but you can write and revise your drafts wherever.

If you find yourself stuck by either tone or writer's block, try drafting the book in your email client. Put one section's title in the subject line of a fresh email and address it to a friend who knows what's going on. And then, in the body, simply type out the shortest possible explanation or justification of the subject line — that's your first draft of that section. This can help escape the mental baggage of "writing a book" and get you refocused on the bit that matters: delivering useful knowledge.

Stop writing for an anonymous crowd; imagine yourself writing to a specific individual who you know, and who wants your help. Stop trying to sound smart. Use the same tone and language that you would use to explain something to a friend or colleague.

If you feel more comfortable speaking than writing, record the first draft of each section (following the ToC) as audio and use an AI transcription service to inexpensively extract the text. One of the members of our nonfiction authors' community, Brian, has most of his first draft by talking into a headset while bicycling through the hills. Find what works for you.[9]

Again, don't worry if you think your writing sucks. The goal for now is just to get it out of your brain and onto paper, where you can start to examine and improve it.

## Define your schedule, do the work

Although a few rare authors appear to thrive on an impulsive schedule, the more common approach is to pick a time when you'll sit at your desk and then sit there, religiously, even if you aren't getting anything done. You don't have to write, but you aren't allowed to do anything else. Eventually, the boredom outweighs the writer's block and you start typing.[10]

I like to give my best few hours to my books each day, which, for me, begins about an hour (and a pint of coffee) after waking up. I've learned that if I don't do my writing first thing, then I don't do my writing. I avoid checking any messages or alerts until after my day's writing is done — the distraction and drama of email simply undoes me.

Here's how Steven Pressfield describes the ritual in *The War of Art*:

> *How many pages have I produced? I don't care. Are they any good? I don't even think about it. All that matters is I've put in my time and hit it with all I've got. All that counts is that, for this day, for this session, I have overcome Resistance.*
>
> *... Someone once asked Somerset Maugham if he wrote on a schedule or only when struck by inspiration. "I write*

---

[9] Our nonfiction authors' community: writeusefulbooks.com/community/

[10] Boredom is the writer's best friend. I wrote the entire first draft of *The Mom Test* while stuck in a cabin in Bavaria, almost entirely due to the fact that I was bored out of my mind with no internet or entertainment. Likewise for the first draft of *The Workshop Survival Guide*, although surrounded by sand instead of snow.

*only when inspiration strikes," he replied. "Fortunately it
strikes every morning at nine o'clock sharp." That's a pro.*

Tendayi Viki, a friend of mine, wrote three award-winning business
books in three years alongside a full-time job and young kids, simply
by waking up early enough to put two undistracted hours into his
books each day.[11] Two hours is plenty, but you've got to carve it out,
defend it, do the work, and then show up again tomorrow.

The first draft is just for you. But for the second and third drafts,
you'll want to begin rereading, refining, and designing an Engaging
reader experience.

---

[11] Watch my full interview with Tendayi Viki at: writeusefulbooks.com/viki/

# CHAPTER 4

# Create an engaging reader experience by giving it all away

From a reader's perspective, your book is a multi-hour journey experienced as *value received over time spent*. If too much time passes before arriving at the next piece of meaningful value, a reader's engagement drops and they'll drift away.

Designing a strong reader experience means deciding exactly how to pace and where to place your book's major insights, takeaways, tools, actions, and "a-ha" moments. It's the difference between a page-turner and a grind and is how you nail requirement #3 of DEEP: Engagement.

## What keeps a reader reading

Readers aren't buying your useful book for its storytelling or suspense. They are buying it as the solution to a problem or a path toward a goal. They'll stay engaged for as long as you are regularly and consistently delivering on that promise.[12]

---

[12] I should probably now mention the apparent counterexample of Malcom Gladwell, author of hugely successful nonfiction, who makes heavy use of both storytelling and suspense. The mundane explanation is that, despite their marketing, Gladwell's books are built as pleasure-givers, not problem-solvers, and that he is writing mainly to entertain, not educate. In Gladwell's own words: "I am a story-teller, and I look to academic research [...] for ways of augmenting story-telling." (Excerpted from his appearance on NPR's *Brian Lehrer Show*: permanent.link/to/wub/gladwell.) If you're

I recently threw away a book I had been very excited to buy and read. On its cover, it promised to explore various entrepreneurial conundrums through the lens of ancient philosophy. The writing was accessible, funny, and charming. But after twenty pages, I still hadn't *learned* anything. The authors seemed to believe that their job was to act the clown and *entertain* me rather than delivering the value I had literally bought and paid for. I began skimming faster and faster, hoping to be proven wrong, until finally discarding the book in disgust. Maybe they delivered the value later? I'll never know.

After trashing that one, I picked up the wonderful *Atomic Habits*, by James Clear, which provided the exact opposite reader experience. Upon cracking it open, I immediately began receiving value. I dog-eared each page where I had a major "a-ha moment" — see for yourself the steady drip of insights that kept me hooked and happy:

At least every few pages, you want your reader to be thinking, "Oh wow, I can use that."

In the image above, you'll notice a few chapter-length blocks of unmarked pages toward the second half of the book — those were chapters that simply didn't apply to me. But since I had already received so much value by the time I reached them, my engagement

---

writing a nonfiction *pleasure-giver*, the Gladwellian style is undeniably powerful. But I wouldn't necessarily emulate it for a problem-solver.

was sky-high and I was more than happy to skip ahead and continue reading.

Although a typical reader wouldn't quite be able to define it, they're highly sensitive to a good (or bad) reader experience, and you'll see it hinted at in their reviews and recommendations. For example, here are two excerpts from reviews of *The Workshop Survival Guide* that make mention of the reader experience:

> *I couldn't read more than 1-2 pages without putting the book down and changing my workshop. It was amazing.*[13]

> *Not a page is wasted, no topic lingered on too long, the reading time between each insight is perfectly calculated.*[14]

Your book can be as "boring" as you like; readers will feel engaged and rewarded so long as it regularly delivers the next piece of whatever they were promised on the cover.

When your reader experience is weak, "getting through it" will feel like hard work, and your book will gather dust, half-read on a nightstand. When your reader experience is strong, people will find themself surprised to have devoured the whole book in one sitting, without any sensation of effort or fatigue.

But interestingly, the value isn't always where you think.

## Value Enablers vs. actual value

Confusingly, just because some piece of knowledge is *necessary* doesn't mean that it is *valuable* — at least, not from the reader's perspective.

The most common way to ruin your reader experience is to spend too long on foundational theory before getting to the bits that people actually want. This feels quite natural as an author ("Let's get the theory out of the way") but is grueling to readers.

---

[13] https://www.amazon.com/gp/customer-reviews/R9AIWQ2ADJHPJ/

[14] https://www.goodreads.com/review/show/3941548470

To see how this works, consider teaching the game of chess to a kid. Nearly every adult will start by explaining all the rules, beginning with the pawns, since that's how an experienced player mentally organizes the game. But from the kid's perspective, they're sitting through an awful lot of theory before starting to have any fun. The game's rules are an *enabler* of future value, not *actual* value, and working through them all upfront feels like a long, theoretical slog:

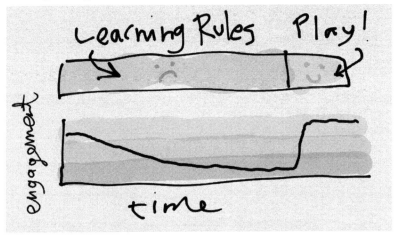

The teacher believes that the eventual payoff will be "worth it." Meanwhile, the kid's Engagement is collapsing. And while you can (occasionally) strongarm a kid into continuing to pay attention despite their own disinterest, your book's readers will simply set it aside and forget it ever existed.

Once you're aware of what's happening, you can restructure the lesson around delivering small pieces of the real value as quickly as possible. In the case of chess, that might mean teaching only two of the six game pieces — the king and castle — and then playing a simple puzzle for checkmate. The learner's Engagement will spike since they're getting what they wanted (to play!), which earns you a bit more of their goodwill and attention. And this, in turn, will allow you to explain another minute or two of theory, play another scenario, and repeat until they've got it all.

As a book, the restructured Reader Experience now looks like this:

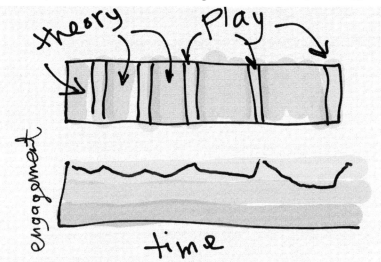

By arranging the content around the *learner's goals* instead of *the teacher's convenience*, the experience stops feeling like a drag and begins to feel easy and engaging. (And as it turns out, this is actually the optimal way to teach chess to kids.)

You want to create the same rapid and consistent delivery of value in your book. And you can visualize it with a slightly modified ToC.

## Visualize the reader experience by adding word counts to your ToC

With one small adjustment, your ToC will become an x-ray view of your book's "takeaways over time," allowing you to visualize, debug, and improve its reader experience.

You do this by adding word counts to the titles of your sections and chapters, allowing you to see how many words (and thus how many minutes — 250 words per minute is typical) are sitting between any two pieces of value. These word counts will be removed prior to publication, but they're invaluable while the book is in development.

Of course, this only works if you followed the earlier advice of using descriptive titles and plenty of subsections. You want to know the word count per learning outcome (i.e., a specific takeaway or insight), not the word count per "topic."

You'll use the marked-up ToC to detect three major weaknesses in your reader experience:

1. A slow start (how many words before the first major piece of value?)
2. Long slogs (lengthy, back-to-back sections without big "a-ha" moments)
3. Fluffy sections (anything with high word count relative to its value)

Once you've spotted potential issues, all three problems can be resolved through a mix of rearranging, editing, and deleting.

For example, in the below snapshot from an early version of this guide's ToC, the two underlines mark sections with suspiciously high word counts relative to the value of their takeaways, suggesting that those sections may want to be aggressively shortened:

CHAPTER 2. Non-fiction as a problem-solving product (4000 words)

Problem-solvers vs. pleasure-givers (170 words)

Problem-solvers are stronger products (270 words)

How a book fails (550 words)

What keeps a reader reading (950 words)

Desirable / Effective / Rewarding / Readable / Polished (300 words)

Word of mouth can anticipated and designed for (340 words)

When word of mouth meets marketing (320 words)

Bestsellers vs. back catalog (1070 words)

It's easy to get stuck in the weeds of a lengthy manuscript and to lose sight of the big picture. Using your ToC in this way will ensure that you're investing your effort into the most impactful places.

# Increase value-per-page by deleting the fluff

Given the typical reading speed of 250 words per minute, cutting 10,000 words (while maintaining the value) saves 40 minutes of your reader's time. Consider how it feels to spend an extra 40 minutes in traffic on the way to the same destination. Don't put your readers through that.

Even if it's only a brief section, finding some way to reduce its word count by 50 percent will double its value-per-page, and your reader will receive twice as many insights per minute of their time. That's a big deal.

Stephen King once said that throughout the writing process, he ends up deleting twice as many words from each book as he leaves in. My experience has been similar. Early drafts of *The Workshop Survival Guide* were 120,000 words (eight hours to read). And what a joy when I finally managed to delete more than half, launching with 55,000 words (three and a half hours). *The Mom Test* went through a similar 50% haircut down to 30,000 words (two hours' reading time).

Deleting whole chapters is mainly about scoping ("Oh, they don't actually need this!"). Deleting anything smaller than that is about a mix of editing and reader experience design.

Throughout the writing process, maintain a separate "cutting room floor" document to paste and preserve all the chapters and sections that you cut from the main manuscript. It's not wasted work; it's part of the process, and those deleted bits will often reappear later as part of your content marketing.

Your early drafts already contain plenty of value. The challenge isn't to add more good stuff. It's to delete all the fluff that's delaying readers from getting to it.

# Front-load the value

The likelihood of your readers recommending your book is based on the amount of value they've received before either finishing or abandoning it. And they're most likely to abandon at the start.

So if you withhold value at the start of your book — either intentionally or accidentally — then you end up frustrating your readers and decimating your word of mouth.

Nonfiction authors make this mistake *all the time* via the inclusion of lengthy forewords, introductions, theoretical foundations, and other speed bumps that come from a place of author ego instead of reader empathy.

You've got three main ways to front-load your book. We've touched on some of these already, but to put it all in one place:

1. Can you delete or reduce the front-matter (foreword, intro, bio, etc.)?
2. If your book begins with value-enablers (theory, context, foundations, etc.), can you rearrange it to insert pieces of real value far earlier?
3. If your whole book is building up toward a grand conclusion or set of tips, can you simply start with the big reveal?

The third approach is the most controversial. Authors often feel that by "giving it all away" too soon, readers will take the goods and run. But I haven't found that fear to be justified. *The Mom Test* delivers most of its big ideas in the first three chapters (about 7,500 words or thirty minutes' reading time). The rest of the book is really just supplemental detail for folks who need a bit more guidance around putting it into practice. Every page is valuable for beginners, who read it cover to cover. Meanwhile, more advanced readers are able to quickly get the value and then move on, grateful that I haven't wasted their time. This structure has done wonders for both engagement and word of mouth.

We already covered the second tactic (of rearranging or inserting pieces of value within the value-enablers), so let's turn to the always reliable third option of simply deleting everything that comes before the first big piece of value. One of my favorite examples of this is from Derek Sivers's *Your Music and People: Creative and Considerate Fame.*

Here's the book's full introduction. Notice how it shares the bare minimum information required to establish basic credibility and context, and then gets out of the way:[15]

*This book is entirely about you and your music. But I use some of my stories as examples.*

*So here's my context, as short as can be, to set the stage for the book.*

*Since I was 14, all I wanted was to be a successful musician.*

*First I graduated from Berklee College of Music in Boston.Then I got a job at Warner/Chappell Music Publishing in New York City. There I learned a ton about how the traditional music industry works. I'll tell you about that soon.*

*Then I quit my job and became a full-time professional musician. I played over a thousand shows of all types. I was also a session guitarist and side-man, then I ran a recording studio, booking agency, record label, and more.*

*I started to see the music business from the other side. I found out what it was like to be on the receiving end of musicians' music. I became friends with successful people inside the music industry, and heard their perspective.*

*I saw thousands of musicians succeed. So I paid attention to how they did it.*

*That's when I started writing my observations in this book. I felt like a spy, giving you the report from the inside, telling you how to get in. Now listen up, and I'll tell you everything I know.*

---

[15] Used here with permission. Find all of Derek's books at: https://sive.rs/#mybooks

Upon reading that introduction, I knew I was holding something written by an empathetic author who was putting the reader first.[16] When I asked Derek about it, he said:

> *It's funny, I felt bad that my intro was even that long! I kinda wished I had none at all.*

The faster you can begin delivering your book's core value, the happier (and more engaged) your readers will be.

## Too long vs. too short

I don't mean to suggest that a lengthy book is always a bad thing. It's only bad if it's longer than it needs to be. Josh Kaufman's *The Personal MBA* weighs in at nearly 500 pages, but every page is dense with value. Nine years after publication, it has become a back catalog classic and soared past a million copies sold.

Still, it's worth noting that lengthier books are slower and more costly to create. A book that's twice as long might easily require five times longer to edit and perfect, while still selling for the same price (and costing more in printing fees). If you have so much to say about a topic, why not consider breaking it into two separate titles?

A paperback can start to feel a bit too thin below about 100 pages, which is somewhere around the 20,000-word mark. But rather than artificially pad out the *words*, it's better to increase the *pages* via thoughtful layout. This makes it feel more "booky" without unnecessarily taxing the reader's time. For example, there are shockingly few words in the category-breaking best-seller *Business Model Generation* by Osterwalder and Pigneur. And yet, thanks to its heavy use of helpful diagrams, illustrations, and creative typography, it feels undeniably substantial.

You can also reframe a book's brevity as part of its value. Alex Hillman did just that with *The Tiny MBA: 100 Very Short Lessons about the Long Game of Business.* Judging by its count of either words or

---

[16] And incidentally, he also self-published and sold $250k worth of books before even publicly launching. He promptly gave it all to charity. Good dude. Learn more at: https://sive.rs/250k

pages, it's short — very short! But since that conciseness embodies the book's exact promise, brand, and message, it ends up working brilliantly. The same is true for Oxford University Press's *Very Short Introduction* series. Small enough to fit in a back pocket and quick enough to read on a commute, these books have been wildly successful.

A book should be as long as is necessary to convincingly deliver on its promise, but never any longer.

## Revise into a third draft and prepare for beta readers

All the stuff we've talked about in this chapter begins to apply from your second draft onward. The very first draft is just about brain-dumping it onto paper. You only start thinking about the reader experience once you're diving back in to rewrite it. But give yourself a little vacation first. A week away from the manuscript between drafts will do wonders for your perspective and sanity.

From the second draft onward, I like to follow Hemingway's approach of rereading while writing:

> *The best way is to read it all every day from the start, correcting as you go along, then go on from where you stopped the day before. When it gets so long that you can't do this every day, read back two or three chapters each day; then each week read it all from the start. That's how you make it all of one piece.*[17]

This does cost more time during the writing, but saves far more time during editing, so I consider it a win. However, if you're prone to endless fiddling and second-guessing yourself, then you'll do better to maintain the strict division of "write first, edit second."

---

[17] This advice is excerpted from one of Hemingway's letters to a young writer who appeared unannounced at Hemingway's door in 1934 after hitchhiking to Key West. For the full story and more, check out *Hemingway's Boat: Everything He Loved in Life, and Lost*, by Paul Hendrickson.

While doing these revisions, focus on the big-picture issues of structure, clarity, and reader experience. Try not to worry about every little problem with grammar, typos, and wordcraft. Spend more effort tightening the earlier sections than the later ones. A strong start can keep folks going through a weaker ending, but a strong ending can't save a disappointing start.

Even after the third draft, the manuscript still won't be anywhere close to perfect. That's okay — it only needs to be coherent enough for a sufficiently motivated beta reader to muddle through and mostly figure out what you're trying to say. Spending the time to make it "perfect" at this point would only be wasted effort, since it's still likely to get torn up and reinvented throughout beta reading.

If you feel that you're losing perspective, try printing it all out on paper, stepping away from your screen, and bringing the paper manuscript to a pleasant cafe or garden. Changing your context can allow you to see old problems with fresh eyes, and reading it from front-to-back can help you notice major repetitions, inconsistencies, and slogs.

If your content divides clearly into standalone parts, you can move faster by honing only the first bit and beginning beta reading on that while you continue preparing the next piece of the manuscript.

You'll sometimes spend a full day painstakingly writing something that you delete the very next morning, which can feel like sliding backwards. But rest assured, it's a healthy and natural part of the process. Here's author and writing guru Delilah Dawson on how to think about the second and third drafts:

*Revisions are not copy edits; they are major surgery and they suck.*

*I didn't understand this one for the longest time. I would hork up a first draft, turn back to page one, and start hunting for typos, feeling smug. Don't do that. That's like digging up a lump of coal and spit polishing it in front of Tiffany's.*

*... Don't read it like it's your precious perfect baby darling. Read it like it's your worst enemy's magnum opus and your job is to expose its every tragic flaw. ... If you get bored reading it, so will your audience.*[18]

Reread it. Revise it. Restructure it. Refine the reader experience. Front-load the value. Remove the chapters and sections that don't apply to your ideal readers.

Just remember that your goal at this stage is *not* to finish a perfect book. The immediate goal is to create something just barely coherent enough for your beta readers to begin working through. Speaking of which...

---

[18] This excerpt is the seventh tip of Delilah Dawson's 25 tips for aspiring fiction authors: permanent.link/to/wub/dawson.

# CHAPTER 5

# Finding and working with beta readers

Beta readers are neither paid professionals nor kindhearted friends. Rather, they are actual, honest-to-god readers who want what you're creating so badly that they're willing to endure an early, awkward, broken manuscript just to get it.

Since beta readers are *real* readers, they can offer real insights, which come from three places:

1. What they say in their comments (qualitative insights)
2. Where they begin to become bored, start skimming, stop reading, and stop commenting (quantitative insights)
3. How they apply the book's ideas in their lives (observational insights)

Taken together, these three types of data will guide you toward a final product that people love.

I find working with beta readers to be the most satisfying stage of writing a book. It's a direct connection to the people you set out to serve and is when the book finally begins to exist in the world as a standalone, value-creating product.

In terms of where it fits within the traditional process, beta reading begins *after* the third-ish draft, but *before* any sort of professional editing. If you're using a developmental editor, they'll get involved while beta reading is still happening, offering an expert perspective to complement the feedback from your readers.

By the end of beta reading, you'll have a DEE_ book (Desirable, Effective, and Engaging) that's ready to advance to the final tasks of Polishing (the missing 'P').

## Begin beta reading while the manuscript still has problems

The biggest mistake with beta reading (apart from not doing it at all) is to wait too long to start, having already spent hundreds of hours on detailed editing and refinement. This is firstly a waste of time, because all that fine work will be torn up as soon as you need to change it. And more subtly, you'll receive *more* helpful feedback by showing a *less* polished product.

Consider what would happen if I asked for feedback on a beautiful oil painting that I'd clearly poured huge amounts of time into. You'd almost certainly just compliment it, perhaps offering some small, inconsequential suggestions to show that you're paying attention. After all, it's practically finished, so how could I even use your big ideas? And given the effort I've already invested, my ego is likely to be all tangled into it, so you'll want to be supportive even if you don't exactly adore what I've made. Whereas if I asked for thoughts on a rough, ugly sketch that took only minutes to create, you'd feel far more comfortable saying that you just don't get it, allowing me to catch and fix its big problems.

To borrow a quote from Reid Hoffman, entrepreneur extraordinaire and founder of LinkedIn:

> *If you're not embarrassed by the first version of your product, you've launched too late.*

Although Reid's advice doesn't quite apply to the final launch of a *finished* book (since it's relatively difficult to update once published), it applies 100% to exposing the pre-launch manuscript to beta readers. If you're completely proud of it, then you've waited too long.

# How beta reading works — how many and how often

Beta reading runs in iterations of 2-8 weeks: the first one or two weeks to gather the bulk of the feedback, and the remainder to work that feedback into a new revision. After each iteration, the manuscript will get stronger, and its problems will get smaller. You'll start by fixing chapters and end by fixing paragraphs.

I aim to find a new set of 3-5 deeply engaged beta readers per iteration, which typically requires inviting 12-20 people who claim that they'd love to read it. Roughly half of them won't even open the document, and another half will submit approximately one comment before giving up. So expect to invite about four times the number of potential readers as you hope to end up with. (Finding these people is less difficult than it sounds — more on that in a moment.)

Early on, each batch of readers will run into a major obstacle that essentially prevents them from continuing (usually either massive confusion or boredom). But that's what you want! So long as they've succeeded in identifying the next set of book-killing problems, they've done their job. As such, you don't want to try to "force" people through the whole book via guilt trips or nudges. Their disinterest *is* the data — it shows you what's next to be fixed.

In the first round of beta reading for *The Workshop Survival Guide*, not a single person made it through even the second chapter. As we edited, rewrote, and refined it over subsequent months (adding new beta readers at each step), we could see folks progressing further and further until nearly everyone was reaching the end and receiving the book's full value.

Consequently, the earlier iterations tend to be faster, because you only need to improve the chapters that people actually got through. Plus, in the early iterations, you're less concerned with prose and minor errors, so you can be more reckless with your edits (for example, relocating an entire chapter without worrying about whether the transitions and cross-references still make sense).

You'll rarely be able to reuse beta readers across multiple iterations. This is partly because they've already given you a lot of their time, and partly because the helpfulness of their feedback degrades on subsequent reads. Having graduated from the context of a first-time reader, they'll end up commenting on tone and typos instead of the big-picture priorities like whether they want it, whether it works, and where they get bored.

How many iterations are required? It depends. In general, the more time you've already spent teaching the book's material, the less time will be required for beta reading. *The Mom Test* felt fairly solid after only two rounds of beta reading. Whereas *The Workshop Survival Guide*, which I hadn't taught as much, took six. And this guide, which I hadn't taught at all before starting, required even more.

If you need a timeline, plan to run at least two full iterations of beta reading (which should take one to four months, depending on how quickly you can do each rewrite). But if your schedule allows for it, you'll ideally continue iterating and improving until your beta readers have shown you that you're finished.

## Your beta readers will show you when you're finished

Your book will never feel as perfect as you'd like. There's always something else to fiddle with or improve. So you'll need to draw the line somewhere, and your beta readers can help you decide where's good enough.

Three strong signals that your manuscript is "finished" and ready to be Polished:

1. It feels easy to recruit new beta readers, since they want what you're offering (Desirable)
2. Most of them are receiving the value and reaching the end (Effective and Engaging)
3. At least some of them are bringing their friends (the recommendation loop is running)

If one or two of the above are true, you're on the right track. Once all three are true, you'll know that your manuscript is ready to be a book. And not just *any* book, but an uncommonly excellent book that can soar on reader recommendations.

Of course, this idealistic advice must be tailored to fit your life's constraints. You're likely working with a finite supply of time, energy, and enthusiasm. Or you may be dealing with a deadline or trying to launch in time for a big marketing opportunity. It's good to have a line in the sand. Eventually, further iterations deliver diminishing returns, and you've got to get it out there sometime.

I launched *The Mom Test* with more than two hundred serious typos because (1) I was losing my mind and (2) a conference had agreed to give away five hundred copies if I could deliver them on time. So I called the book good enough and then did five rapid updates post-launch to fix its most egregious errors for future customers. That was a stressful time and I don't recommend doing things this way, but sometimes life gets complicated. With *The Workshop Survival Guide*, Devin was having his first kid and I was losing ground in a footrace against burnout, so we knew that we needed to finish it then — or never.

If possible, spend the time to make your book as brilliant as it can be. And certainly don't fall into the trap of skipping beta reading altogether; it's too important for that. But do run the process with an eye toward acknowledging your personal constraints, maintaining your momentum, and getting it out the door before you run out of steam.

## Finding and managing beta readers

Finding these readers isn't as daunting as it might feel. A six-week iteration cycle, for example, would only require stumbling across somewhere between two and four new potential readers each week to find the 12-20 "interested" (and the 3-5 "actual") that you require for that iteration.

So where do you find them? In general, it's no different from how you found your reader conversations (Chapter 3). As a reminder:

- ○ Begin by pinging friendly first contacts (including everyone who enjoyed talking to you during reader conversations)
- ○ Mention the book as "your thing" whenever someone asks you what you've been up to
- ○ Plant a flag online by adding the book to your email signature, as well as any relevant social networks, profiles, and sites

Additionally, after you've done at least one or two iterations, you'll want to begin doing some pre-launch marketing. While this is mainly in pursuit of launching with part of your seed audience already in place (see Chapter 7), it also allows you to invite the most eager fans to become beta readers.

If you happen to have the benefit of a pre-existing audience and/or a waiting list of potential readers, I suggest inviting only a subset into the manuscript at the start of each iteration. This will allow your list to last through the whole process instead of burning out on one iteration.

If you can't find *any* readers, consider that a nudge to do a bit of soul-searching about whether you're writing the right book for yourself and your readers. Sometimes even a small adjustment to the scope can unleash the excitement from all sides, making you more willing to put your work out there, and making your readers more eager to jump into it.

# Pick the right tools for live commenting and negative feedback

Before inviting your first beta readers, you'll need to:

1. Move the manuscript into a tool that allows for live feedback
2. Add instructions explaining the most helpful types of feedback that a reader can give

Your choice of feedback tool is crucial. I foolishly tried to get feedback for *The Mom Test* by sending out PDFs, which was a nightmare. I had no way to know who was engaging and would often receive weeks of silence, occasionally followed by an email containing thousands of comments about a now-outdated version. Plus, integrating the comments back into the master manuscript is an unbelievable time-sink. You really don't want to be exporting and emailing anything.

You can still *write* in your preferred tool of choice (Word, Scrivener, Google Docs, etc). But once you're ready for beta readers, copy/export the manuscript into a cloud-hosted tool with live commenting. Google Docs is free and works well enough for this task. Set the permissions to allow people to comment/suggest, but not edit, and optionally disable their ability to download or duplicate the document. You can either invite them individually (for tighter access controls), or simply make the manuscript public-by-default and then share the link.

Alternatively, Devin and I have built a tool specifically for better beta reading called *Help This Book*,[19] which is designed to gather more (and better) data as well as to help you make better sense of it. I used it for this book:

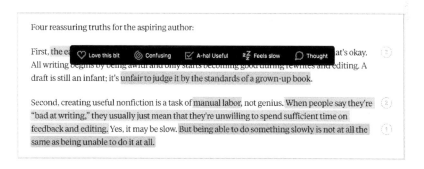

You also need to tell your beta readers what type of feedback you

---

[19] Although I'm admittedly quite biased, I found *Help This Book* to be an incredible improvement over alternatives. It nudges readers toward providing the most useful types of feedback and also gives you a nice author dashboard to make sense of it all. Give it a try at helpthisbook.com.

need. Otherwise, they'll spend all their time flagging typos when you're still trying to figure out the core content. Here's what this looked like for *The Workshop Survival Guide*:

**Dear review reader:**

Thanks for taking a look. This review is **not** about spotting typos (there are lots). Instead, the most useful feedback is about stuff like:

- Where you get confused or lost or have an unanswered question
- Where you disagree, or have different experiences
- Where you start to get bored and feel like skipping ahead or giving up
- Anything you find especially interesting or helpful

You can leave inline comments in the Google Doc (easiest for us, if possible), or just email comments to rob@robfitz.com or devin     @     .com.

Huge thanks :)
—Rob & Devin

Including these sorts of instructions will vastly improve the quality of feedback received.

Whichever tool you use, ensure that it's on the web (so you don't need to deal with versioning pandemonium) and that you've told your readers how best to help you. It's simple stuff, but important.

## Save the most influential readers for last

Most people will only review your manuscript once. Which means that if a potential beta reader is especially influential — as either a testimonial or an evangelist — then you may want to delay inviting them until your manuscript is fairly strong.

You can't *expect* anyone to do any evangelism on your behalf, and you shouldn't try to force it, since that would only succeed in burning bridges. But given that you've written something DEEP and useful, you'll have a fair shot at unlocking their support without even having to ask.

If an influential beta reader does mention that they love what you've written (whether directly to you, via their comments in the manuscript, or publicly on social media), then you're well-advised to request a testimonial for your book's cover or Amazon page. Beyond that, keep them in the loop about your launch timelines and send them a few copies — signed, if possible — once the book is published.

Devin and I messed up basically everything about the launch of *The Workshop Survival Guide* (more on that in Chapter 7). But one thing we did right was to get signed copies into the hands of fifty influential review readers. The logistics took some time, but it wasn't difficult — we just found their emails, said we wanted to send them a new book, and asked for their postal addresses. We asked for nothing in return, but some of them went out of their way to help us anyway.

If you can't find the right people before launch, don't panic. *The Mom Test* launched with zero testimonials (which was admittedly a mistake on my part). But as the book grew over subsequent months and years, unsolicited testimonials started appearing from influential people, and I simply updated the cover and promotional materials to include them. When you've built a book to last, you're able to breeze past a lot of early blunders.

# CHAPTER 6

# Gather better data, build a better book

Now that we know how to find and manage beta readers, let's shift our attention to *learning* from them, as well as how to detect the elusive, hidden signals of boredom and disengagement.

(All the reader comments displayed in this chapter are from real beta readers of my books — mostly from *The Workshop Survival Guide*.)

# Evidence of value, insights, and takeaways

I've been surprised to discover that I can rarely predict which specific parts of a book will be most valued or enjoyed. But once the best bits have been identified, I can easily go through the rest of the manuscript and add more moments like them.

The first comment above shows that I'd hit some value. Sometimes the value is where you expect, and you can simply move along, happy that the section is working as intended. Other times, readers will find major value in what you thought was a minor side point, which might prompt you to emphasize it further or even expand it into its own section.

The second comment shows that I'd found a tone and style that the reader loved. (In this particular case, it was a matter of shifting from saying "here are all the options" to "here's what you should do.") After confirming this with a few other people, I went through the book and employed that style a whole lot more.

Identifying the value can fundamentally change a book. In the early versions of *The Mom Test*, I had included a silly mock conversation to demonstrate how getting feedback tends to go wrong. I felt a bit sheepish about its goofiness and had only used one such example. But beta readers *loved* it, saying that it solidified a normally abstract concept. So I ran with it by adding absurd — but useful — example conversations to nearly every chapter of the book. And although the occasional grumpy reader might disagree, these mock conversations are a big reason that the book ended up working. And they started out as an accident. I never would have known they mattered without my beta readers.

Even when a comment isn't directly actionable, it's still awfully nice to hear that folks are getting value. When editing becomes a grind, a few encouraging words can make all the difference:

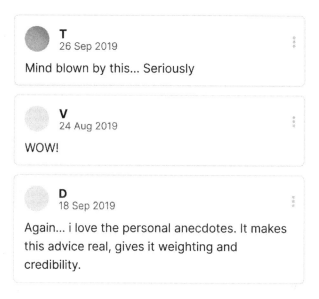

**T**
26 Sep 2019

Mind blown by this... Seriously

**V**
24 Aug 2019

WOW!

**D**
18 Sep 2019

Again... i love the personal anecdotes. It makes this advice real, gives it weighting and credibility.

Being cheered on by such wonderful readers keeps motivation high. But of course, there's more to reader feedback than just good news.

# Confusion, skepticism, and missing information

I also want to know where I've missed the mark and left my readers confused or skeptical:

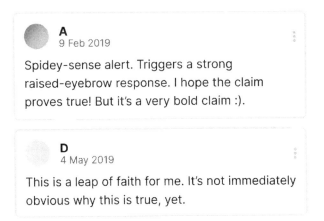

These first two comments reveal that a piece of my core argument was flimsy. Fair enough. I went back to add clearer justification and tighten it up.

The next two comments show that at another point, I had wandered too far into the weeds and lost my readers:

**H**
9 Feb 2019

This section threw me off. I thought I missed something between the earlier section and this one. I think bc the previous section made me think you were gna explain more about how to think through / approach creating a workshop - whereas this overview is rather technical and about stuff I don't know how to do

When a reader seems confused, pay attention to that precious signal. It's easy (and tempting) to respond with an eye-roll while thinking, "C'mon, pay better attention!" But that only serves to preserve the problem.

Far better to think, "A-ha, my book has a weakness; let's see if I can fix it so nobody else gets lost in the same way." Even if you're technically correct and have explained it earlier, if one reader gets stuck, then others will as well, hindering your recommendation loop.

## Factual inaccuracies, oversimplifications, and overgeneralizations

If any of your beta readers are subject-matter experts (or even enthusiastic amateurs), their experiences can help identify where you're overgeneralizing, oversimplifying, or just plain wrong.

**A**
9 Feb 2019

I do the same, but with a minutes-since-start / minutes-until-end timer. Musch more power to react while on your feet.

This first comment points to a case where I had presented my personal preference (for workshop timekeeping) as if it were the One

True Solution. But by doing so, I had both oversimplified the problem and overgeneralized my approach. Thankfully, a beta reader straightened me out, and we ended up including his suggestion in the final book.

The next comment — from the same reader — highlights a spot where I had attempted to make a major point via sloppy reasoning. Glad he caught it:

**A**
9 Fed 2019

This feels a bit circular, like: "a great skeleton is great". I was expecting something more actionable and specific.

Similarly, a diverse set of readers will also help you catch places where you've been inadvertently insensitive, rude, biased, or offensive.

## Delete the sentences drawing unnecessary drama

A small number of your minor sentences will attract a disproportionately large amount of criticism, confusion, drama, and debate. You may want to delete those sentences.

Early drafts of *The Workshop Survival Guide* made the claim that some of its techniques could be applied in a more traditional classroom environment. And while I still believe that's technically true, it's also true that school teachers are working under far more demanding and difficult constraints than freelance facilitators. As such, teachers ended up feeling that those sections were either trivializing or disregarding the challenges of their profession. In a perfect world, I would have been a skilled enough writer to make my point without offending anyone. But since I wasn't that skilled, I instead deleted each and every mention of the traditional classroom environment, replacing them with examples and anecdotes from the freelance workshop world. Having done so, not only did the problem disappear, but school teachers actually started liking the book.

Of course, you'll sometimes need (or want) to hold the line. In the words of legendary writer Cormac McCarthy:

> *Don't worry too much about readers who want to find a way to argue about every tangential point. ... Just enjoy writing.*[20]

I do a bit of both. I'll first attempt to clarify and fix the issue. If I can't, and if the point is educationally essential, then I'll accept the outrage of some small percentage of readers in exchange for being able to better serve the rest. But if the point is tangential or nice-to-have, then I'm dashing to delete it.

## Fall in love with negative feedback

Negative feedback can feel like a real kick in the pants, especially if you've just poured dozens of hours into your umpteenth rewrite.

But far better to hear it now — while you have a chance to fix it — than to be blindsided later by the slings and arrows of outrageous Amazon reviews. The moment you start disregarding or rationalizing negative feedback is the moment you lose your ability to improve your book.

Still, there's no denying that it's tough. Despite knowing that your readers are going out of their way to help you, it's easy to start taking things personally.

One of my all-time favorite beta reader interactions was composed of just two comments. The first said, "I am literally so excited to be reading this." The second, just a few pages later, said, "This is fluff — I don't like fluff." And then she left and never came

---

[20] This excerpt is from McCarthy's advice to authors of scientific papers and applies equally well to useful nonfiction. Other tips include: "Decide on your paper's theme and two or three points you want every reader to remember," "Limit each paragraph to a single message," "Don't slow the reader down," and "Avoid footnotes because they break the flow." Hmm. Full article at: permanent.link/to/wub/mccarthy

back. And she was right! I lost that reader, but she helped me make a better book.

Bec Evans, founder of Prolifiko, an author education and coaching program, describes the mindset for accepting tough feedback:

> One bit of advice I give writers is to see each draft as a hypothesis or experiment: your job is to gather data to test that version of the manuscript and figure out what's wrong with it.
>
> If it fails, it doesn't mean that you have failed, but only that the current experiment has. So you redesign it. Shift your emphasis off the personal and back toward the product. Perspective is everything!

Steven Pressfield, author of the *The War of Art*, says:

> The problem isn't you. The problem is the problem.

Pressfield's meaning here, at least as I understand it, is that it's never you against your readers. It's you *and* your readers working together against the problems in the manuscript.

If you ever become tempted to argue with a beta reader, do yourself a favor and step away. Get a good night's sleep or take a week's vacation. Attempting to "win" in a comment thread is clear evidence that you've started taking things a bit too personally and could use some time away. Plus, even if you do manage to convince them, you've done it outside the manuscript, so other readers will still stumble over the same issue.

Of course, this doesn't force you into blindly obeying every single suggestion — especially if the feedback is coming from someone who is outside your ideal reader profile. Use reader feedback as a lens to see what's going wrong, and then come up with your own way to fix it.

Toward the end of editing *The Workshop Survival Guide*, I found myself with a cohort of beta readers whose comments drove me near to madness. It seemed like these readers were intentionally *not getting it.* I was already pretty worn down and could feel my ego firing up defensively, so I closed the document and took a vacation. Upon my return, I dug in and realized that this group of readers all happened to be non-native English speakers, and that I had been over-relying on fancy idioms to deliver core concepts. I simplified the language and the confusion stopped.

The most helpful feedback of all is about where readers are becoming bored. But that data isn't just laying around in plain sight — you must learn to detect it.

## Detecting boredom, abandonment, and the hidden analytics of reader engagement

The challenge with detecting boredom is that most readers are too polite to explicitly mention it. Or they won't even notice what's happening, blaming themselves for "not paying attention" or "feeling tired" when the problem is actually a failure of reader experience design.

The best way to detect boredom is to identify where readers are quietly giving up and abandoning the book. If readers are jumping ship in Chapter 3, for example, then it suggests that either Chapter 2 was a low-value grind (thereby exhausting them before they got to the good stuff), or that Chapter 3 is.

There's no perfect way to detect this, but you can make a fairly accurate estimation by noticing where a reader's comments stop. Using comments as a proxy for engagement isn't perfect data, but it's close enough to point us in the right direction.

Yes, it's possible that the reader's life may have just gotten crazy and that they suddenly ran out of time. But that's a risk for your finished book as well. Distracted and busy readers are a fact of life. And if your manuscript was sufficiently valuable, they would have made the time.

With each subsequent iteration of beta reading, you should see people getting further through the manuscript, showing that the reader experience is improving and that "boredom" is decreasing. Here's how we visualize it in *Help This Book*:

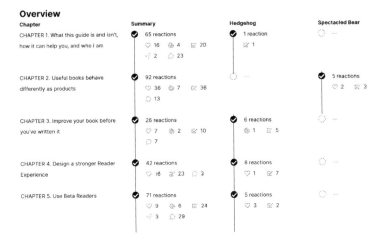

Once you know where readers are disengaging, you'll need to take a guess about what caused it and how to fix it. Nine times out of ten, the problem is low value-per-page in the surrounding areas.

As such, the answer is almost always to wade into the surrounding sections with a chainsaw, aiming to slash their word counts by half or more. Engagement drops — and boredom rises — due to long slogs through low-value pages. You'll never cure boredom by adding more words, which only dilutes the value further. Deletion is your savior.

This is yet another reason to invite *actual* beta readers instead of just pressuring your friends or hiring a professional. Friends and professionals feel obligated to finish the manuscript, which denies you the invaluable data of where they're getting bored and wanting to give up.

## Follow up to see whether the book actually worked

Readers' comments on your manuscript will reveal their experiences *while reading*. But if your book intends to change their behavior, mindset, skills, work, or life, then you'll also need to watch what they're doing in the weeks after they've finished reading. And since they'll no longer be commenting inside your manuscript once they're out in the world, you'll need to follow up with them.

After each iteration of beta reading for *The Workshop Survival Guide*, Devin and I would each reach out to a few of those readers with a brief follow-up email. It was always hand-written but sounded like this:

> *Hello, huge thanks for all your amazing comments and feedback. We really appreciate it and wanted to return the favor by making ourselves available to help with any questions or problems. Have you had a chance to design or run a workshop since reading it? Did anything not work? Are you stuck on anything? We'd love to help.*

And while not everyone took us up on the offer, enough did for us to glimpse how they were actually applying — or failing to apply — what we had been trying to teach them.

Follow-up conversations aren't necessary for every topic. But if you're writing something that requires the reader to act, then going beyond the comments is invaluable.

People will only recommend your book if it has successfully touched their lives. "Sounded good in theory but didn't work for me" is a death blow to an otherwise recommendable book.

## Begin pre-sales once the book is mostly working for beta readers

I'd suggest beginning pre-sales during the second half of beta reading, once you're fairly confident that the structure is correct and that the knowledge works. This timing allows you to begin building your seed audience (and earnings) in advance, but without the risk that your timelines will slip too much.

I've twice fallen into the trap of pre-selling too early. The first time, I began selling an eventually abandoned "book" while it was still just a table of contents. After promising the world, taking people's money, and doing five ineffective rewrites, I was forced into an awkward set of apologies and refunds upon realizing that I couldn't deliver on what I had promised. Some years later, with *The Workshop Survival Guide*, we began pre-sales in the earliest stages of beta reading, only to discover that we needed to do a full restructure and would (significantly) miss our launch dates.

You've got two potential approaches for selling your book before it is launched:

1. Pre-order — they pay today and get it eventually, after it's finished
2. Early access — they pay now and get the current manuscript immediately, plus updates along the way and a finished copy once it's done

Both options are fine, and the choice mainly comes down to how many sets of eyes you want on the pre-launch manuscript (plus your comfort-level with technology, since the second option is more complex to set up).[21]

## Finishing and polishing the book

Once your beta readers are signalling that the book is Desirable, Effective, and Engaging, you've got two overlapping tasks:

1. If you haven't already started, begin your seed marketing
2. Add the P to DEE by polishing, professionalizing, and publishing it

We'll cover seed marketing up next, in Chapter 7.

---

[21] If you're self-publishing through Amazon KDP, you can easily accept pre-orders (but not early access) for the Kindle version, which helps gather verified reviews and launch at #1 in your categories. To offer full early access (or pre-sell paperbacks), you'll need a different way to collect your customers' information and money. The simplest option (at the time of writing) is gumroad.com, which is built to sell digital files and also allows you to collect shipping information if you want to send out paperbacks. (Although you'll still have to organize the paperbacks yourself — see the Appendix for details.)

As for polishing it, the biggest task — and the one that feels most writerly — is to hammer your prose into shape through detailed, repeated editing passes. Remember all those times I told you to ignore the little problems until later? Now's the time to fix them. Tighten and clarify the language. Remove extra words. Print it out and read it from front to back. Follow your sense of craft.

Depending on your book's content, you may also want to organize some sensitivity readers (for inadvertent marginalization or bias), expert reviewers (for fact-checking), and a legal review (usually only needed if you're worried about potential libel or fair use issues, or to insure the book as a business asset).

If you are working with a publisher, they'll guide you through all of this. If you're self-publishing, hiring a little bit of professional help is highly recommended. Nearly everyone should pay the few hundred dollars for a good copy editor (for sentence-level improvements) and proofreader (for typos and grammar). A developmental editor is a larger, more expensive luxury if you're still stuck on the bigger-picture stuff.

Beyond the prose itself, self-publishing authors will also need to work through a laundry list of production tasks: interior layout, cover design, print on demand, and more. These tasks are somewhat tedious, but aren't difficult. (See the Appendix for a checklist and additional guidance on doing them.)

And now's the time to start your seed marketing. Ideally *before* launch, not after it.

For most authors, "marketing" is a scary word. However, since you've written a *useful* book, there happen to be four exceptional marketing options that stand out above all others. Let's look at each.

# CHAPTER 7

# Seed marketing to find your first 1,000 readers

Before organic growth is able to kick in and carry you forward, some number of happy readers must have already received massive value from your book. These early evangelists are called your seed audience (or seed readers). Once you've found them, you can step back and allow organic growth to take care of itself. But until then, you're on the hook for doing manual, hands-on marketing.

How many readers do you need to find? Personally, I aim to get any new book into the hands and hearts of 500-1,000 seed readers before taking my foot off the gas, which could require anywhere from a few weeks to a few months.

April Dunford (author of the already-mentioned *Obviously Awesome*) approaches seed marketing differently, committing to a stretch of time instead of a number of readers. As she memorably told me:

*Launch is a year, not a day.*[22]

A year-long launch might appear a terrible burden, but I see it in a brighter light. A useful book's long-lasting relevance relieves the pressure of the do-or-die launch. With a broader time horizon, minor mistakes and mishaps aren't such a big deal, and the urgency

---

[22] April Dunford gives loads more detail about her launch strategy in my interview with her. It's dense with knowledge and very worth watching: writeusefulbooks.com/dunford/

evaporates. You'll still need to do the work, but you can do it at your own pace.

Recommendability adds considerable leverage to your marketing efforts. For example, I manually seeded 800 readers for *The Mom Test* and then, over the next few years, organically sold another 50,000 copies through word of mouth. Meaning that each copy I manually marketed eventually led to another 60 copies sold (and growing). That's a solid multiplier and is, incidentally, how to flip book marketing into a profitable equation.

Successful marketing isn't really about marketing at all — it's about product design, testing, refinement, and ensuring that you're delivering real value to your readers. But assuming you've already got that recommendable foundation in place, it's time to get tactical.

## Four marketing options for useful books

I've wasted tons of time experimenting with wacky, situational book marketing gimmicks. Fortunately, a small set of techniques appear to work well, and to be reliable, repeatable, and relatively time-efficient.

Some of these options won't apply or appeal to you, which is fine. You only need one good approach to seed your book. So if any of the sections or ideas in this chapter feel annoyingly irrelevant to your situation, just skip ahead to the next one.

My top four suggestions for seed marketing (in no particular order) are:

A.  Digital book tour via podcasts and online events (most scalable)
B.  Amazon PPC (pay-per-click) advertising (easiest but unscalable)
C.  Event giveaways and bulk sales (fastest if you have the contacts)
D.  Build a small author platform via content marketing and "writing in public" (most reliable and valuable, but time-intensive)

I seeded *The Mom Test* primarily with event giveaways (no ads) and *The Workshop Survival Guide* almost exclusively through PPC ads (no events). *The Mom Test* was seeded in days, whereas *The Workshop Survival Guide* took months. When I eventually returned to actively supporting *The Mom Test* after a five-year hiatus, I relied mainly on the podcast book tour. For the book you're now reading, I'm (finally) spending the time to build a proper author platform.

I mention these different approaches and timelines to reassure you that there's no magic bullet and that it's okay to play to your strengths, preferences, and constraints. I've used all four options in the past. Each has different trade-offs, but they all work.

If I were starting over with absolutely zero resources, reputation, or connections, I would rely mainly on the fourth option — writing in public to build a small author platform — complemented by Amazon PPC ads. But since you're probably not starting *completely* from scratch, you'll want to be familiar with all four approaches, since one or another might offer an easier win.

## A) Digital book tour via podcasts and online events (most scalable)

Here's Chris Voss, author of the three-million copy bestseller *Never Split the Difference*, when asked about the value of physical book tours:[23]

> Book tours, in and of themselves, are the biggest waste of time you can possibly do. I did a couple early on just 'cause they said I should, even though I'd heard they were a waste of time.

It's true. Commuting around the world to personally promote your books is an unbelievably poor use of your time.

---

[23] From Voss's brilliant interview on episode 313 of Anna David's *Launchpad Publishing* podcast: permanent.link/to/wub/voss

Instead, get better results in a twentieth of the time by sitting at home in your pajamas and doing a *digital* book tour.

Podcast hosts and digital event organizers are in the business of finding interesting, valuable content for their audiences; if they believe you can provide that, they will gladly have you on their show. And given that you happen to be the author of a useful book, this becomes a fairly straightforward proposition.

The hardest gig to get is the first. After finding that first opening, additional invitations tend to follow. The more talks you've given, the more hosts will hear you, and the more opportunities will arrive in your inbox. Over time, you can spiral your way up from the obscure to the influential.

Here's Voss again, in the same interview, talking about how he got started promoting his book and when it received its big break:

> *My son and I, you know, we're hard workers from the Midwest. Tell us how hard to work and we're going to try and outdo it.*

> *I remember hearing about Tony Robbins's early days, when he would schedule up to three talks a day. So our goal was, we gotta start talking to people. It doesn't matter who it is. Don't rely on the publishers — we had marketing people, we'd hired a PR firm — don't rely on them. Outwork them.*

> *So we started reaching out to podcasts. Who are the influencers? I'm going to hunt them down. And I don't care [about their size]. Again, start small.*

> *The real game changer was [getting on] Lewis Howes's podcast [The School of Greatness]. Lewis Howes is huge and it hit hard. Then the other podcasts all jumped on because they saw Lewis.*

*The only time you should go outside [to talk about] the
book itself is opening day, day one, and get on TV. You're a
news story, so get on the right TV show, which ain't that
hard. Cause if your book is right for the TV show, they
want you on because they need the news. But no physical
book tours.*

*We really went after podcasts. And then constantly giving
content, you know, as much content as possible. I think the
podcasts made the biggest difference.*

An unusually well-attended keynote presentation at an in-person
conference might have two thousand people in the room, requiring
multiple days of preparation and travel. Whereas you can crush those
numbers in an afternoon with one decent podcast or a few smaller
ones.

That being said, most podcasts are extremely small. In 2019
there were 750,000 active podcasts, with a median of 141 listens per
episode.[24] That's not exactly a crowd, but it only takes an hour,
you've got to start somewhere, and it all adds up. And as Voss
mentioned above, one big show can completely change the game.
Start small, but keep an eye on working your way up toward the
bigger shows.

If you're not a natural with public speaking and interviews,
compensate with extra prep. Here's Derek Sivers again (who
appeared in Chapter 4 with his reader-friendly author bio), on how
he excels — against his natural inclinations — as a podcast guest:

*I'm a disappointing person to try to debate or attack. I just
have nothing to say in the moment, except maybe, "Good
point." Then a few days later, after thinking about it a lot,
I have a response.*

*... I'll tell you a secret. When someone wants to interview
me for their show, I ask them to send me some questions a*

---

[24] Podcast statistics: permanent.link/to/wub/podcast-data

*week in advance. I spend hours writing down answers from different perspectives, before choosing the most interesting one. Then when we're in a live conversation, I try to make my answers sound spontaneous.*

*People say that your first reaction is the most honest, but I disagree. Your first reaction is usually outdated. Either it's an answer you came up with long ago and now use instead of thinking, or it's a knee-jerk emotional response to something in your past.*[25]

I've listened to many of Derek Sivers's appearances, and I deeply appreciate the extra effort he invests in preparation. Because it ensures that my time, as a listener, is rewarded with dense and thoughtful value. Sivers describes himself as a "slow thinker." But with time to reflect, he's a deep thinker, and he's found a way to use that. Play to your strengths.

The digital book tour allows you to scale rapidly beyond your own reach by leveraging the larger audiences of well-established podcasts and well-promoted events. But it's obviously not for everyone. So let's now turn toward the *easiest* option: Amazon's underappreciated book ads.

## B) Amazon PPC ads (easiest but unscalable)

For most useful books, Amazon's native book ads will hugely outperform the ads on any other platform. When someone searches on Google or Facebook, they're looking for information or entertainment. When they search on Amazon, they're uniquely open to the idea of paying for a book. The intent-to-purchase is unparalleled.

Unfortunately, profitable ad campaigns don't scale as far as you like, since there are only so many clicks available and they become increasingly expensive as you try to capture more of them. As such,

---

[25] From Sivers's essay, "I'm a very slow thinker." https://sive.rs/slow

you'll typically use them as an addition or complement to one of the other marketing approaches.

But, if you don't mind waiting a few months, ads can (eventually) build your seed audience all on their own. After completely botching our launch for *The Workshop Survival Guide*, Devin and I relied on this approach. The ads sold 25-100 copies per month at a moderate profit, returning $2-3 for every $1 spent while slowly building a seed audience. Within a few months, word of mouth had kicked in and organic sales were 10x higher than ad-driven sales. Due to our relaxed approach, the book hasn't reached anywhere near its full potential. But given the other priorities in our lives at the time (a baby for Devin and burnout for me), it was the right choice for us.

Interestingly, PPC ("pay per click") ads work better for self-published authors than those who are published traditionally. This is because a self-published author receives higher royalties per copy sold, allowing them to pay higher per-click prices while still turning a safe profit. (This is also one of the reasons to resist pricing your book too cheaply — it hinders your ad campaigns.)

If you're familiar with other advertising platforms, you may be surprised to learn that you're largely powerless to customize what appears in your Amazon ads. Your book's cover and title/subtitle *are* its advertisement — you can't just add a compelling photo or catchy tagline to make it more clickable. So if your cover is illegible and your title/subtitle mysterious, then your ads won't work.

To get started, expect to spend a few days learning the basics and then about four hours per week (for the first few months) managing, optimizing, and improving your campaigns.[26] Begin with Amazon's automated campaign suggestions — they're a solid starting point. Avoid the "Kindle Lock Screen" ad type — they don't convert anywhere near as well as the other options (at least for the type of nonfiction this book is concerned with).

Amazon takes two months before paying royalties, so your cash flow will be delayed. But you receive the analytics immediately, allowing you to pause or adjust unprofitable campaigns before

---

[26] Beyond Amazon's own educational resources (which are excellent), the best information about getting the most from Amazon ads is from Dave Chesson at kindlepreneur.com.

burning a hole in your wallet. Begin testing the campaigns at a low budget (less than $20 per day) and only increase the spend once it has proven profitable. The ad dashboard looks like this:

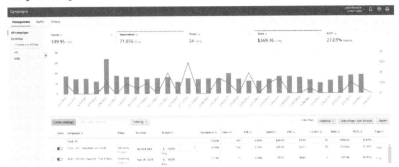

The above screenshot demonstrates both the strengths and the shortcomings of book ads. On the one hand, it's a little bit of free money ($369 in sales from $99 of spend) and 24 extra seed readers. But it's also not much of either. (Meanwhile, we sold 500 organic copies that same month via word of mouth — remember that all of these seed marketing strategies are about *starting* organic growth, not replacing it).

For certain topics, you may have better luck with ads on other platforms. For example, I've heard of authors in the fashion industry doing six-figure royalties primarily via Instagram and TikTok ads. If your topic is a perfect fit for another platform, then it may be worth experimenting with ads outside of Amazon. But they're extremely situational.

In any case, I strongly suggest playing with a few Amazon ads as soon as your book is up for sale. It's not a magic bullet, but it's certainly an extra bit of ammunition.

## C) Event giveaways and bulk sales (fastest)

Although I would never suggest wasting time by setting up a stall and trying to *sell* books at an event (the few dollars per hour you'd potentially earn is almost certainly not worth the opportunity cost), you should jump at any chance for your books to be given away to an event's worth of ideal readers.

In fact, if I had to choose how to benefit from a large event, I would much rather do a giveaway (to every attendee, not just one or two copies) than be their keynote speaker.

To seed *The Mom Test*, I gave away 500 copies at one event (they covered printing costs of £2.50 per copy), 200 at a second (they paid discounted bulk prices of £10 per copy), and marketed 100 myself via content marketing (which we'll look at next), for a total of 800 seed readers.

Tendayi Viki told me that he seeded his first book — which went on to be an award-winning best-seller — in a similar way:

> With [my first book], The Corporate Startup, I didn't really have an audience, so that's why I was hopping onto [other people's] platforms, getting them to allow me to show up at their workshops and conferences.

> The "official" launch of the book was at the Lean Startup conference in London, and I personally bought 250 copies of my book to give away to jumpstart it. I just stood there — there was a queue, people were arriving, and I was signing the books and giving them away.

> I only had to do that once. But as someone who was starting out, that was something I had to do. After that, those folks recommended it to other people.

> Of course, if you give away 250 boring books, it might have a negative effect. Eventually, you're always relying on word of mouth. After that first marketing push, there's nothing else. People have to be saying, "Oh yeah, I used this book, and it worked."[27]

For giveaways to be worthwhile, recipients need to be as close as possible to your ideal reader profile — they don't count if they won't love it.

---

[27] Watch my full interview with Tendayi at: writeusefulbooks.com/viki/

Additionally, the event must be able to ensure that all attendees actually receive a book, which typically means either putting them out on chairs before folks show up, including them in the gift bags, or leaving a giant pile of them (with no friction, queue, or delays) at a key junction or gathering point.

For online events, your book must be linked/included directly in an email sent to all attendees. In the best case, the event pays you directly for the appropriate number of digital licenses, optionally at a steep discount. The point here isn't about the money, but the fact that the event will be more motivated to distribute and promote something that they've paid for. Less optimal, but still better than nothing, is for the event to send out a special digital purchase link in one of their attendee emails. You'll get close to 100% penetration with a direct giveaway, and 10–20% penetration with a good email purchase link.

To find willing events, you must first understand that from their perspective, even a "free" book is never free — any sort of giveaway carries a high reputational risk by acting as a tacit endorsement. So the organizer must believe, first and foremost, that the book is useful to their attendees.

One slightly sneaky trick is to research relevant events while your book is still being written, and coax a few organizers into becoming beta readers. This is a smaller request (asking for their time instead of their reputation) that allows you to begin demonstrating value and building a relationship.

To do a physical giveaway, you'll need physical books. However you decide to handle the printing,[28] a typical paperback will end up costing you roughly $2–5 per book, depending on the number of copies ordered and the page count of each. However, you'll rarely need to pay for printing out of pocket. Once an event has decided to bear the reputational risk of giving away a book, they'll typically also be able to find the budget to cover costs (or more).

If you're in the business of paid consulting or speaking, you can easily upsell clients by adding their logo to the cover and a custom foreword to the innards. I've sold five or ten thousand of these

---

[28] See my guide on bulk printing options: writeusefulbooks.com/guides/bulk-printing

custom-branded books to a mix of corporations and universities, and they absolutely love it. Bundling books into your normal client services also offers some creative pricing/negotiating power since you can steeply discount one or other component while still ending up with a higher overall fee. Also, clients can sometimes pay for your books and services from two separate budgets, which helps unlock more overall discretionary funds.

But what if you're starting without any sort of connections, contacts, or reputation? In that case, you're down to getting your book out there the "real" way, which is to repurpose your manuscript into its own marketing.

## D) Build a small author platform via content marketing and "writing in public" (most reliable)

Between beginning and finishing his first book, Arvid Kahl grew his author platform from zero email subscribers and 400 Twitter followers to several thousand subscribers and 8,000 followers. That's an achievable size of platform to build alongside writing a single book, and was enough to launch Arvid's book, *Zero to Sold*, to #1 in its Amazon categories and deliver $20,000 in royalties within the first six weeks of publication. As Arvid explained to me:

> *All of my "marketing" was just sharing the work I was already doing on the manuscript.*
>
> *You can write your book in public, chapter by chapter or section by section, and just continually release these things to an ever-growing audience of people. Nobody will compile it into a book and release it without you.*
>
> *Doing that consistently, every single week, will build an audience whether you like it or not.[29]*

---

[29] From my interview with Arvid: writeusefulbooks.com/kahl/

And while "writing in public" won't always be applied quite so literally, Arvid's overall approach to platform-building is simple, time-efficient, and replicable by any author. The crucial insights:

1. You can reuse the book's content as its own marketing
2. You can begin doing this very early, even with rough drafts and tiny excerpts

Austin Kleon — whose four nonfiction books, including the wonderful *Show Your Work: 10 Ways to Share Your Creativity and Get Discovered*, have sold over a million copies — puts it perfectly:

> *Once a day, after you've done your day's work, find one little piece of your process that you can share. If you're in the very early stages, share your influences and what's inspiring you. If you're in the middle of executing a project, write about your methods or share work-in-progress. If you've just completed a project, show the final product, share scraps from the cutting-room floor, or write about what you learned.*
>
> *Don't say you don't have enough time. We're all busy, but we all get 24 hours a day. People often ask me, "How do you find the time?" And I answer, "I look for it."*[30]

Stop trying to figure out how to "market your manuscript" and start realizing that your manuscript *is* the marketing.

Of course, this doesn't necessarily mean that you can (or should) do a pure copy/paste/publish of your book's contents onto the internet. Many of your book's sections may depend on the context of what came before, requiring some extra framing, explanation, or adjustment when excerpted.

---

[30] More advice from Kleon in this article: permanent.link/to/wub/kleon (and in his books of course)

In terms of practicalities, you'll need to make four decisions:

1. Where to post — including both relevant online communities and your own audience
2. What to post — how to adapt your preexisting work into high-value nuggets of standalone content, which could include sharing:
   a. Your drafts, excerpts, and deletions
   b. Your research, references, and learnings
   c. Your process, progress, and behind-the-scenes
3. When to schedule your posts — a repeatable process to reduce the time cost and emotional drain
4. How to capture interest — respectfully converting internet strangers into direct contacts

Consistency is key, so try to figure all of this out before you get started. It's hard to be consistent if you're always improvising. Let's take a peek at the practicalities of each decision.

## Make a list of places to share

If you've already built your own blog, newsletter, or relevant social media following, then that's your default sharing destination. But if you're getting going from nothing (or want to supplement your existing audience), then you're still in luck, because your readers have almost certainly gathered themselves into one or more online communities around their goals and interests.

Most online communities will welcome submissions that are some combination of helpful, educational, interesting, inspiring, and sincere. Most will have explicit submission guidelines about what's okay to share, as well as their own implicit "culture" of how they treat self-promotion.

Once you've found some relevant groups (either by Googling or by asking your readers where they hang out online), spend some time researching each community's "culture" and compiling your findings into a list for future reference.

Then, whenever it's time to share something (e.g., a valuable idea, quote, excerpt, or example), you can simply scan your list and decide where it best belongs. My list (for this book) begins like this:

| Aa Community/audience | # Members | ☰ What they like | ☰ Priority? |
|---|---|---|---|
| In⬛ | 100000 | Case studies, behind-the-scenes, tutorials, marketing | ✳ ✳ ✳ |
| /r/w⬛ | 1200000 | Inspiration, celebration, writing quotes, productivity, tools | ✳ ✳ |
| Rob's Twitter | 12000 | The business of books, behind-the-scenes, milestones | ✳ ✳ |
| Rob's YouTube | 900 | Interviews, anecdotes, stories, advice | ✳ ✳ |
| Rob's LinkedIn | 2000 | Business advice, revenue examples, encouragement, milestones | ✳ |
| W⬛ | 5700 | ? | ? |
| 2C⬛ | 45000 | Royalties, efficiency, productivity, marketing hacks, tools | ✕ |

Once you've decided *where* to share, it's time to figure out *what*.

## Share your writing, drafts, and excerpts

Although a good book is clearly more than just a pile of articles and tweets, a manuscript does contain the raw material that can be harvested into that sort of marketing content.

Is it scary to post your work-in-progress? Sure. So how do you get started? By starting. Here's the viewpoint from Jeff Gothelf, four-time author and founder of Sense & Respond Press:

> *Building an online presence, at its core, is a simple strategy: start writing. Share your experiences, expertise, knowledge, wins, and perhaps equally as important your losses.*
>
> *Originality will emerge from continued publishing. You'll find your voice. You'll find your audience. You'll get better at telling your story and they'll appreciate it even more.*[31]

---

[31] Watch my full interview with Jeff Gothelf at: writeusefulbooks.com/gothelf/

Here's the thing: you're already doing the work. You're already writing a manuscript. Let it work for you.

Gary Vaynerchuck, founder of the content marketing powerhouse VaynerMedia, has championed a similar strategy to produce hundreds of pieces of content per day by repurposing and reusing snippets from a single piece of lengthier source material. Here's their process:[32]

1.  Create "pillar content," which is a larger piece of work that can be clipped, excerpted, and highlighted (such as a podcast interview, conference talk, training video, or your book's manuscript)
2.  Repurpose it into "micro content" like articles, quotes, images, stories, remixes, rants, etc.
3.  Distribute across social media, communities, and content platforms

Following Gary's model, your manuscript is not one piece of content — it's a thousand.

Take your whole draft and pull out the highlights as articles or videos. Then break those excerpts down even further and post them as short-form snippets somewhere else. Reuse, repurpose, and reap the rewards.

One easy option is to simply screenshot some piece of the manuscript, add some highlights or commentary, and share it. This sort of content is infinitely repeatable and requires only moments to create. For example, here's a recent post featuring a highlighted excerpt from the very first draft of this chapter:

---

[32] GaryVee's content model: permanent.link/to/wub/garyvee-content

Maybe you dislike Twitter, or maybe the style doesn't work for your audience — that's fine. Don't get too hung up on this specific example. The point is to find some way to repurpose the work you're already doing into something relevant to your potential readers.

As another example, here's a longer a post I made to reddit's "r/writing" community, largely composed of excerpts and snippets from my manuscript:[33]

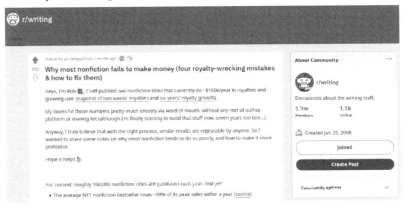

---

[33] The full reddit post if you're curious: permanent.link/to/wub/reddit-example

This post took half an hour (since it was already mostly written in the book), got 122 upvotes, and led to a fair number of new customers and seed readers.

A related option is to share the stuff you've deleted. While writing and editing, maintain a second "cutting room floor" document. Whenever you delete a paragraph, section, or chapter from your main manuscript, paste it into the second document. That pile of deprecated drafts and detritus is a perfect source of raw material for your content marketing.

Like all things marketing, doing it once is not a magic bullet. But once you've overcome the friction of setting up your process and learning the ropes, it doesn't take too much time or effort to maintain. And if you do this sort of thing consistently alongside writing your book, it's all the marketing that you'll ever need to do.

## Share your research and references

You might also share the research you're doing. If, say, you're writing about the lessons of history, you'll be bound to come across all sorts of interesting facts, anecdotes, and references. Share them! Even if it's just a small link or quote, that's fascinating stuff to the same people who will eventually want to buy your book.

This applies doubly to original research. While working on this guide, I interviewed a bunch of other authors. After realizing that I shouldn't be keeping those wonderful conversations to myself, I began asking permission to record and share them.

I'd then post the highlights to YouTube, social media, my own site, and any other relevant destinations, like this:

If you're going to do the research anyway, why not allow it to serve double (or triple) duty as marketing?

## Share your process and progress

Here's Austin Kleon (*Show Your Work*) once again, on adding your own behind-the-scenes experiences into the marketing mix:

> Traditionally, we've been trained to regard the creative process as something that should be kept to ourselves. We're supposed to toil in secrecy, keeping our ideas and our work under lock and key.
>
> But human beings are interested in other human beings and what other human beings do. By sharing our process, we allow for the possibility of people having an ongoing connection with us and our work, which helps us move more of our product.[34]

---

[34] From Kleon's blog: permanent.link/to/wub/kleon

For many nonfiction topics, readers will be just as intrigued by your day-to-day process as your written output. If you were writing for lawyers, why not share your ongoing learnings and surprises around book law and publishing contracts? Or if you were writing for entrepreneurs, they'd likely devour data about your marketing and earnings. A creative audience might enjoy hearing about your own struggles and breakthroughs, and a fitness crowd might subscribe for unguarded discussions of your exercise plans, pitfalls, and progress.

Once the book is out there, you can use its own success as a fresh excuse to talk about it, which April Dunford calls a "momentum launch." Did you hit #1 on Amazon with your pre-order? Grab a screenshot and tell your story. Earn your first dollar in royalties? That's a story. Get your fifth perfect review? Tell people! This works especially well for books about business/money/marketing, but can also be creatively applied to many other topics.

For his second book, *The Embedded Entrepreneur*, Arvid Kahl began using the momentum launch even earlier, sharing feedback and insights from beta readers as a way to both promote his book and recruit even more readers. As a result, he ended up having over 500 beta readers helping him with the manuscript, and he built a happy seed audience as a side-effect.

These sorts of announcements also act as a great hook to get yourself invited onto podcasts. After all, the journey to the milestone makes for a great story, and podcast hosts are always on the search for stories worth sharing. Not long after sharing a quick screenshot of my Amazon royalties dashboard, I was invited onto several great podcasts to talk about my experiences. Putting yourself out there won't guarantee that you'll get lucky. But refusing to do so most certainly guarantees that you won't.

As numerous creatives have noted over the years, the optimal career strategy is simple:

*Make things and tell people.*

Again, you don't need to do *all* of this. Some options won't resonate with either yourself, your content, or your audience. But you don't need to do all of it. One repeatable approach is plenty. To review the options of what you might post:

- ○ Share your writing, drafts, and excerpts
- ○ Share your research and references
- ○ Share your process and progress

Of course, you also need to force yourself to put it out there, which requires a system and a schedule.

## Get accountable by creating a content schedule

I'll admit that I don't particularly enjoy the marketing side of things. As such, I'll take any excuse to delay doing it, which often slips into doing nothing at all.

To hold myself accountable and become more consistent, I made a little checklist that I work through (and then reset) for each week of seed marketing. Yours will look different, but here's mine:

Weekly seed content marketing

☐ One new knowledgebase article *(modified book excerpt or answer to a reader question)*

☐ Three tweets or threads *(highlighted excerpts, big ideas, examples, behind-the-scenes)*

☐ One YouTube video *(reader Q&A, author interview, highlight from earlier video)*

☐ One LinkedIn post *(repurposing any of the above)*

☐ One social news post *(to any relevant community, repurposing any of the above)*

Arvid Kahl approaches accountability from a slightly different angle. He told me:

> I started with just an occasional blog post. But then I realized that I'm a very lazy person, so I started my newsletter as an accountability scheme for myself, since it forced me to send something out every week.

*I'd write a chapter or a section of my book, post it as a blog post, send out the same thing as a newsletter, and then read it aloud — plus a little extra commentary — as a podcast episode.*

*The most important thing I learned was consistency.*

*Thank goodness that tools exist to make this easy. I went away for a vacation, and we did a digital detox with no phones or computers. So, the week before, I spent a few hours queuing up all the stuff I wanted to send out while I was away, and it all happened without me.[35]*

Putting your early work out there is too emotionally demanding for a loose, "I'll do it when I feel like it" sort of approach. If you wait until the "right time" arrives, you may be waiting forever.

Find some way to stay accountable: use my checklist; use Arvid Kahl's approach of public accountability; or use Austin Kleon's simple requirement of, "Once a day, after you've done your day's work, find one little piece of your process that you can share." But do use something.

## Capture emails to convert "interest" into "audience"

Assuming that your book isn't already available for presale (in which case, you would just link your marketing directly to your purchase page), you'll want to capture interest by getting people's email addresses.

In terms of value-per-follower, email is orders of magnitude better than social media.

The "normal" option requires setting up your own newsletter (as well as having a website and the ability to drive traffic to it via content marketing). But there's also a low-tech alternative that

---

[35] Plenty of tools exist to help with content scheduling. At the time of writing, hypefury.com and buffer.com are two popular options. Again, Arvid's full interview is at: writeusefulbooks.com/kahl/

works surprisingly well, which I'll mention toward the end of this section.

If you're collecting emails while the book is still under development, then I suggest offering a multi-tier signup that allows people to tell you whether they'd like to get involved in beta reading or whether they'd prefer to wait for the finished version — this helps you make the most of your fledgling audience.

Of course, many readers already suffer from "newsletter fatigue" and are justifiably skeptical about signing up for yet another. The solution is to offer them an enticing digital gift — called a "lead magnet" — in exchange for their signup. The gift is usually some sort of digital knowledge that is valuable for them to receive but free for you to give away. In the case of a useful book, the lead magnet could be an exclusive bonus chapter, video tutorial, case study, research report, templates, worksheets, or anything similar.

Here's how Ryan Holiday, one of today's best book marketers, approached it:

> With my book The Daily Stoic, we built a 40,000 person email list by sending out one additional free meditation every single morning.
>
> This is an incredible amount of work — basically one additional book written per year — and I do it totally free.
>
> BUT — it helped the book spend five weeks on the Wall Street Journal list. And without really any other marketing, the book now sells 1,000–1,200 copies per week.[36]

When I returned from my multi-year hiatus to begin optimizing sales of The Mom Test, I spent a few days mimicking Holiday's approach (on a far humbler scale) by creating a short, five-part email series

---

[36] Ryan Holiday's full case study and advice is at: permanent.link/to/wub/ryan-holiday

(with each email explaining one common mistake of customer interviews), which roughly 5,000 people have now trickled through.

If you'd prefer to skip setting up your own site and newsletter, the clever folks at the software company Basecamp recently found a solution. Instead of using a signup form and newsletter to gather interest for their new product, they asked people to simply send an email expressing interest (to a dedicated address), which eventually led to more than 150,000 inbound messages.

Alex Hillman, author of *The Tiny MBA*, wondered whether this approach would translate to books (spoiler alert: yes) and ended up launching his own that way, cruising to an easy #1 pre-sale rank on Amazon. Here's how he described the first twenty-four hours of his "email me if you want it" experiment:

> When folks started asking how to preorder my new book, instead of whipping up a landing page, I decided to try this alternative opt-in technique. There is no landing page or website for the book. Just a few photos and an email address!
>
> I sent out a few tweets telling people to email me if they were interested, plus one post each on Facebook and Instagram, for a total of 358 likes, 9 shares, and 25 comments. In 24 hours, 90 people had emailed to request a pre-sale link. And more keep coming in.
>
> It's a lightly manual process, but it also means that I get to read every email folks send. Which brings me to the two best parts.
>
> First, if you think getting waiting list signups feels good, getting actual emails with personalized messages from people who are excited to buy your thing is NEXT LEVEL. I'm hearing from folks I haven't talked to in ages. People

*are asking to buy multiple copies as gifts for friends and coworkers.*

*Second, when it comes time to launch, I plan to actually reply to all of the emails that folks sent in. I know that my emails will reach their inboxes because they're being sent by a human. Plus, my message will show up as a reply to an email that they sent ME, which is safely prioritized as "not spam" as well as being more likely to stand out in their inbox.[37]*

That's a spicy set of benefits. Especially for something as easy as setting up an extra email address and telling people about it.

However you decide to do it, find some way to (respectfully) capture emails in order to convert today's audience into tomorrow's customers.

## Pick whichever path feels easiest

Of the four options for seed marketing, building and maintaining an author platform is by far the most time-intensive. But in the long term, a supportive audience is incredibly valuable. It's a permanent, compounding asset that will travel with you from project to project for as long as you continue doing interesting work. Whether that feels like a worthwhile investment of time will depend largely on what you plan to do next.

If you're planning to finish the book and then move on to a completely different industry, then you can likely seed your audience more time-efficiently with the other three approaches. But if your book is intended as the cornerstone of the next stage of your career or business, then absolutely, yes, invest in the platform. It will become a multiplier to everything else you do.

Apart from that, follow whichever path feels easiest. If you're already doing client work, then bulk sales will probably feel "easy." If

---

[37] This excerpt is from Alex Hillman's post at: permanent.link/to/wub/hillman-email. I also interviewed Hillman about it: writeusefulbooks.com/hillman/

you're already doing public speaking or teaching, then event giveaways or the digital book tour will seem most natural.

And if you ever see a low–hanging opportunity that's a perfect fit for your readers, then try it! A book about travel, fashion, or lifestyle, for example, might do brilliantly on Instagram and TikTok, even if those are not viable channels for most nonfiction titles.

With an eye toward your future goals and interests, you might also choose to invest in doing it the hard way. If you've always wanted to write a blog, grow a YouTube channel, become a public speaker, or master advertising, then why not use your book as an excuse to start toward that goal?

As mentioned, there are no magic bullets. Building a seed audience from scratch will always feel slower than you would like. But once it's done, it's done, and your book can grow from there on its own merits. And to help it along the way, you may want to spend just a little bit of time optimizing it.

# CHAPTER 8

# Optimize for sales and growth

Having already invested the substantial effort required to build something recommendable and long-lasting, spending just 10-50 extra hours on optimization can easily double your overall sales and growth.

These tactics won't help a book *start* selling, but they will help it to sell *more*. The most common and impactful options include:

- Optimizing your Amazon purchase funnel (50%+ sales increase)
- Adding percentage boosts with extra platforms and products (5-20% uplift apiece)
- Turning piracy to your advantage by ensuring that the book acts as its own marketing
- Engaging with and supporting superfans and evangelists (and optionally teachers and trainers)

When I fixed just the first issue — the purchase funnel — for *The Workshop Survival Guide*, sales jumped by 50% overnight, adding more than $10k to that book's yearly royalties. When I applied the full list of optimizations to *The Mom Test* (at around year six, which was admittedly a bit late), sales roughly doubled, adding more than $50k to its yearly earnings, as you can see here:[38]

*The Mom Test* — Yearly Royalties

As a caveat, it's impossible to pin down precisely how much this stuff really matters. Amazon is hedgy with its data, and rigorous experiments are impractical to run. But based on everything I've seen and heard, I believe in it.

Given the potential upside, it's startling to see how little effort authors typically invest in optimizing this side of things. And I get it — upon finishing your book, you deserve to be working your way through a beachfront margarita, not more tasks. Be that as it may, skimping on these final steps risks diminishing the value of everything you've already done.

So let's get started with the easiest, biggest win: your purchase funnel.

## Optimize your Amazon purchase funnel

When first discovering your book on Amazon, people will almost always see it as a tiny thumbnail image of your cover, nestled alongside a bunch of other tempting books.

---

[38] I give more context and discussion of this graph in my 2021 talk at the Nonfiction Authors' Association annual conference. Watch it at: writeusefulbooks.com/nfaa/

Your first challenge is in enticing potential readers to click on *your* cover instead of someone else's. After that, your store page must convince them that your book is, in fact, the best available solution to their current goal or problem.

These two decision-points make up the heart of your Amazon purchase funnel:

1. Getting shoppers to click on your book instead of someone else's (relies on your cover, title, subtitle, and reviews)
2. Getting them to press "buy" instead of "back" (relies on your store page, description, and reviews)

If you already know all this stuff, feel free to skip ahead to the following sections about percentage sales boosts, pricing power, piracy, and enabling superfans. But if you've never thought of your Amazon page as a crucial business asset, then read on.

## A "clickable" cover makes a clear promise that's legible as a thumbnail

When someone searches on Amazon for anything other than your book's exact title, you need to get noticed and clicked. You've only got three levers to make this happen:

○ Your book's cover when viewed as a tiny thumbnail (less than 300 pixels tall)
○ Your title and subtitle
○ The number of reviews and average star rating

That's it. Only the first two are within your immediate control, and the first is *by far* the more important.

Disclaimer: *The Mom Test* doesn't follow this advice (but my other books do). That's my mistake. But it allows us to use *The Mom Test* as an anti-log of what *not* to do. Consider, for example, the top Amazon results for the highly-relevant search of "customer development." Assuming that you hadn't already heard of any of these books by name, you'd be far more likely to click on *any of the other three* instead of mine. Why?

Because their promise is legible at thumbnail size and mine isn't:

Yes, a sufficiently motivated customer could figure it out by reading the subtitle text down below. But most people don't. Most people just insta-click the first cover that looks relevant, which almost certainly isn't mine.

This also impacts your ad campaigns. One of the reasons that we advertise for *The Workshop Survival Guide* and not *The Mom Test* is that nobody can figure out what *The Mom Test* is about by just glancing at its thumbnail. Whereas the promise of *The Workshop Survival Guide* is crystal clear, even when small:

You can easily update and improve your cover after launch. The title and subtitle, however, are significantly more difficult to adjust. Ensure that either title or subtitle is descriptive enough to define who the book is for and what it will do for them.

The reason that *The Mom Test* has ended up succeeding in spite of these mistakes is entirely due to word of mouth. Despite its unclickable cover, enough people have searched for — and purchased it — for Amazon to eventually figure out where it belongs. But I strongly suspect that it would have enjoyed a far faster start if I had followed best practices.

You'll notice that the star rating and number of reviews also feature prominently alongside your thumbnail. Hassan Osman, host of the podcast *Writer on the Side*[39] and author of *How to Get Book Reviews on Amazon Authentically*, suggests that there's a psychological tipping point of credibility at around 20-40 reviews, and that it's worth going out of your way to encourage (authentic) reviews until reaching that number. Reviews serve a powerful double-duty, encouraging people to click to see your book's store page, as well as to buy from it.

## Your store page should sell (not just describe) and you should use every available option

The main "fix" we made to *The Workshop Survival Guide's* funnel was to rewrite a very mediocre Amazon description (that had been copy-pasted from the book's back cover) into something that actually explained the benefits that the reader would receive. We didn't do anything especially brilliant, but just took a moment to apply a few standard principles of copywriting:

- o Speak directly to the reader's situation and goals, explicitly listing the book's promise and benefits to their life, using readers' own words (from reader conversations and beta reading) where possible

---

[39] I appeared on episode 065 of Osman's podcast to talk all things nonfiction. Listen at: writerontheside.com/400k-from-writing-nonfiction-books-with-rob-fitz/

- o  Include more text and detail than you think you should (at least five paragraphs, and arguably more), allowing potential purchasers to continue reading until they've convinced themselves
- o  Use visual callouts (like headers, lists, and bold text) to grab the eye and allow for skimming
- o  If in doubt, start by picking the book's five most compelling learning outcomes (which should be on plain display in your ToC), using those as the sub-headings for your description, and then adding a paragraph of explanation/justification to each — that's a first draft of your description and you can hone it from there

Now, there's obviously an upper limit to how salesy/cheesy you want to get. One hundred percent salesy is probably too much, and zero percent salesy is absolutely too little. Find somewhere in the middle that clearly conveys the benefits and impact of what you've built.

Beyond the main description, there are also several "hidden" sections that most authors (and many publishers) appear to overlook. These include:

- o  Author profile (filled out and linked via *Author Central*[40])
- o  Featured blog posts and videos, if you have them (also via *Author Central*)
- o  Editorial reviews (written by experts but submitted by you, as opposed to the normal "customer reviews")
- o  "Look inside" page samples (created automatically, but can be customized to show the strongest samples)
- o  Additional product images (potentially including more than just a book cover)

The "editorial reviews" section is especially powerful, as it's essentially a gigantic "free text" field in the middle of your product

---

[40] Create and modify your Author Central page via author.amazon.com, which can then be linked to your books.

page that you can use to say anything you want. Amazon does enforce some guidelines, but you can get more creative than you'd expect.

Having filled out (and improved) the elements of the store page that are within your control, you'll also want to do what you can to encourage legitimate reviews.

## You can't "game" reviews, but you can encourage real ones

Reviews create social proof and will meaningfully improve both clickthrough and conversion rates. Furthermore, organic reviews create a powerful flywheel within Amazon's algorithms, improving your book's placement and priority.

Your immediate goal is to get 20-40 verified reviews (for social proof) as well as a steady, organic stream of daily sales and reviews (for Amazon's algorithm).

According to *Launch to Market: Easy Marketing for Authors*, by Chris Fox, there's a hidden "flag" that gets thrown within Amazon's systems after a book has received organic purchases for five days in a row. Having crossed this milestone, your book gains the ability to be recommended as a "suggested product" on other product pages, and is treated by Amazon as being a legitimate, trusted offering. This is based on five consecutive days of *purchases* rather than *reviews*, but it's an illuminating example of how Amazon's algorithm "thinks," and how it values consistency over volume.

The folks at Amazon are well aware that any sufficiently well-platformed author can gather hundreds of reviews by bribing fans with a valuable giveaway, so they ignore these sorts of large, temporary spikes. These incentivized reviews will still be visible (which might be nice for your ego), but they don't seem to influence Amazon's ranking or recommendation algorithms. Whereas a steady stream of daily activity is much harder to fake, and is therefore treated as stronger evidence of a quality product.

One accelerant for gathering the first few "verified" reviews is to launch your Kindle version at the lowest possible price (currently $1.99), which allows you to request a two-dollar favor from people willing to give it a fair look and share what they think. You can even bring that price down to zero — while still maintaining the "verified" tag — if you're willing to launch as a Kindle Exclusive, which lets you discount the Kindle version all the way down to zero while still treating it as a real purchase. Exclusivity is obviously non-viable if you intend to sell your book via your blog or other platforms, but it can be a free win if you were already planning to be Amazon-only. (If you launch with a discount, raise the price as soon as you've received the early reviews — we'll return to pricing shortly.)

If the idea of actively encouraging reviews feels uncomfortable, then fear not: writing something useful is still enough. For example, beyond occasionally mentioning that reviews were helpful, I never explicitly requested a single review for either of my first two books, which are now sitting at 675 and 175 reviews on Amazon, respectively (and another 4,500 reviews on Goodreads). Reviews do matter, but as always, time is on the side of a useful book.

While we're on the topic, let's talk about the dreaded one-star reviews. Here's what Seth Godin has to say about it:

> How to understand it when someone hates what you do?
> When they post a one-star review, or cross the street to avoid your shop, or generally are unhappy with the very same thing that other people love?
>
> It's not for them.[41]

The first one-star review I ever got was from a reader who was *extremely angry* that she had already known everything the book contained. In my view, she ought to have been more frustrated by her own decision to buy a book that she clearly didn't need. But she chose to blame the book, and I can understand that as well.

In a certain way, one-star reviews are an inevitable result of a useful book's success. Once a book has started to make a positive

---

[41] From Seth's blog: permanent.link/to/wub/bad-reviews

impact on readers' lives, they'll begin to wholeheartedly recommend it. And those endorsements will occasionally mislead the wrong people — who the book wasn't written for — into reading it. As a result, they won't receive the promised benefit and will feel swindled.

That's fair, and I'm fine with it. If a book of mine was going to end up having a four-star average rating, I'd much rather it got there via mostly five-star reviews — and a few one-stars — as opposed to entirely four-star reviews. As always, it's better to be loved by someone than ignored by everyone.

## Create percentage sales boosts by adding extra formats, platforms, and support

Having optimized your book's primary store page, you may optionally look to get the book out into more places, in more formats, and to more audiences.

The classic examples of "extra formats" are an audiobook, PDF, and online course. "More audiences" includes selling the book through smaller (i.e., non-Amazon) retailers, as well as doing "partnerships" to tap into other people's audiences. Under the right circumstances, these paths can all be hugely profitable. But far too often, they're a quagmire of lost time.

Let's start by looking at audiobooks, since they'll point us toward how to think about all similar opportunities.

Selling one copy of an audiobook is far less profitable than selling one paperback or ebook. For *The Mom Test*, I earn approximately $17 per paperback ($30 retail price, 55% royalties after accounting for printing costs), $7 per ebook ($10 price, 70% royalties), and less than $3 per audiobook (since they're usually bundled into an Audible subscription). But due to the popularity of audiobooks, and despite driving less than 10% of my total profits, the audiobook represents over 30% of my "readers."

Assuming that you've built something recommendable, offering an audiobook is therefore *extremely* worthwhile since it increases the number of happy readers who are able to recommend the book and fuel organic growth. And surprisingly, an audiobook doesn't cannibalize the other formats as much as you would think, since plenty of people *only* buy audiobooks.

Creating my first audiobook cost approximately 30 hours (ten hours on a failed first attempt, then eight to record the four-hour audiobook and a dozen more on research and fiddling), plus $250 for a freelance audio editor. In return, I got an extra 10% profits and 30% readership.[42]

This same mentality can be used to evaluate many other nice-to-have distribution options for your book:

*Increased reach + increased profits*

*VS.*

*Time cost + financial cost + stress cost*

As a result, not every "good idea" is worth doing. If it sells too few books while costing too much time/money/stress, then your attention is better spent elsewhere.

For example, I was recently asked to create an online course for one of my books, which the "partner" would promote to an audience of 14,000 semi-relevant people. It would certainly sell a few books and create a bit of extra revenue. But it would also cost me 20+ hours to do properly, plus a bit of money and lots of stress. Upon consideration, this opportunity felt quite "expensive" relative to its expected outcome, so I decided to decline and focus on other options. (Although I probably would have jumped on it if I had still been in the seed marketing stage.)

To get your wheels turning about potential opportunities, here are a few ideas that have worked for me to create small percentage boosts in monthly sales (in approximate order of impact):

---

[42] Whenever possible, I'm a strong believer in recording the audiobook yourself. Professional narrators tend to maintain a steady, polished, and consistent tone throughout the entire book, because they don't know what matters. But some points deserve a bit of excitement! And while you may not sound quite as polished as they would, the fact that you know what to emphasize, where to pause, and where to speed up can make a world of difference. But if doing it yourself doesn't feel comfortable or practical, a professional is also fine.

- o Record an audiobook — 20-30% boost to sales, 5-10% boost to royalties
- o Submit the book to more platforms (iBooks, Google Play, etc., or distribute to all of them at once via a tool like IngramSpark or Draft2Digital) — 5-15% boost in total across all non-Amazon platforms
- o For traffic on your own website or blog, sell the book directly as a PDF, MP3, and/or EPUB via Gumroad (or something similar) for 97% royalties — 38% boost in royalties for copies sold on your site vs. Amazon
- o Allow bulk orders for events, universities, and corporations (as discussed in Chapter 7) — potentially huge boost to both profits and audience, especially if combined with consulting/teaching, but relies on networking, sales, and logistics
- o Create a "press pack" (i.e., a credibility brochure for your book) to assist with sales and PR — valuable if you're doing lots of direct sales with universities/corporations/conferences, but pointless if you aren't
- o Translate the book into more languages — proceeds can be significant (it's a whole extra book!) but requires seeding a fresh audience for each language, so it's more involved and time-consuming than it appears
- o Support teachers, trainers, and consultants with worksheets, slide decks, suggested readings, and lesson plans — top priority for academically-viable books, meaningless for others

These activities all have fairly high time costs and deliver only small, percentage-based improvements. As such, you needn't feel pressured to create any of them prior to launch. But once the book is shown to be working and growing? At that point, even a small percentage boost can compound into a significant advantage when your book is made to last.

## Pricing, profit per copy, and situational upsells

My quick advice is to charge $20-30 for your paperback and $9.99 for your ebook. The exceptions are if you prefer to sell a digital upsell bundle via your own site/audience (in which case you can charge *more* for the whole bundle) or to monetize the long-term customer relationship with additional product/service upsells (in which case you can charge *less* for the book).

Useful nonfiction can (and should) be priced somewhat higher than a "typical" book, although it still can't go as high as it deserves. This is partly due to psychological hurdles from consumers about the fair price of "a book" and partly due to industry ecosystem restrictions.

But you should absolutely NOT charge the minimum. Once someone has decided to invest *any* amount of their time and money in a book, the difference between $2 and $10 (or $10 and $20) is negligible. If you can sell an ebook for $2, you can sell it for $10. If you can sell a paperback for $10, you can sell it for $20. This adds up. Plus, charging bargain basement prices signals low value while also reducing the viability of pay per click ads (covered in Chapter 7).

The reason I recommend selling ebooks for $9.99 (as opposed to $20 or $30) is due to Amazon's definitely-not-price-fixing policy of paying 70% royalties for ebooks priced at $9.99 or below, but only 35% for anything priced higher than that.[43] This means that you make zero extra dollars by doubling the price from $9.99 to $20, even if you sell the same number of copies. (If you can continue selling the ebook above $20 at the same volume, then it finally becomes profitable.)

And once you've set the Kindle version at ten bucks, you're essentially forced into price matching with your PDF and other digital versions.

---

[43] The exact "limit" on ebook pricing varies slightly by region and currency and may change over time. See Amazon's latest royalty structures at: kdp.amazon.com/en_US/help/topic/G200634560

However, you've also got two workarounds to create additional pricing power. Both are situational and won't apply for most authors. But they're *extremely* powerful when they do.

The first is to offer "upsell bundles" of additional resources like videos, tools, worksheets, templates, tutorials, and personal support. This requires a delicate balance — going too far can risk feeling as though you are withholding value from your book, reducing it to a lengthy infomercial, destroying the value-per-page, and undermining organic growth. So instead of *withholding*, you're searching for a sensible piece of *additional* or *complementary* value. The book should feel complete and self-contained on its own, while the upsell offers a compelling — but non-essential — bonus for the especially motivated.

A typical pricing scheme is $10-30 for the book, $50-75 to add the digital educational bonuses, and $150-250 for the full set of tools, templates, and time-savers. This feels high for consumers, but is a no-brainer for business customers, who value each hour of time saved at hundreds of dollars.

According to authors I've interviewed who have used this approach, only 10-20% of customers will purchase an upsell, but that's still enough to double the book's overall profitability. You can't really do this via Amazon, so it requires being able to drive meaningful amounts of traffic to your own website.

The second profit-boosting option relies on having (or creating) a business that serves the same sort of people who would read your book. I once heard of a self-published lawyer who paid to have his book featured in London's train station bookstores, spending tens of thousands of pounds to sell a grand total of 500 books. And yet, he said it was the best money he ever spent, because each of those readers spent two hours coming to understand why he was the best lawyer for their needs, and he closed several hundred thousand pounds' worth of work as a result. And although I don't necessarily endorse the lawyer's *exact* approach (it requires deep pockets and a willingness to gamble), the broader point is that if you're able to turn engaged readers into high-value customers, then the actual price and profits of your book hardly matter.

When Alex Hillman told me about his decision to remove *The Tiny MBA* from Amazon and sell it only through his own website,[44] he explained that the long-term value of the customer relationship was a big part of it. He knew that he would sell fewer total copies without the flywheel effect and exposure of Amazon. But he also knew that each copy sold would be 10x more valuable if it arrived via his own website, since he would receive the email address of every buyer, allowing him to stay in touch and let them know about his business's other relevant offerings.

Bundles and upsells can be huge profit-boosters. Just ensure that you write something useful enough to motivate readers to want to learn more from you, and that you've provided them with a way to do so.

As a hidden bonus, a similar set of tactics will also allow you to benefit from piracy.

## Leverage piracy by turning your book into its own marketing

If you make your book available as a PDF, it's going to get pirated. And even if you choose *not* to release it in such an easy-to-share format, once it gets popular enough, someone will still scan all the pages to create a blurry bootleg version.

In fact, one of the very first Google results for "the mom test" is a pirated PDF of the entire book. And here's its top-rated Amazon review:

⭐⭐⭐⭐⭐ **I pirated the book. Stopped reading. Went to Amazon and bought it.**
Reviewed in the United States on May 1, 2018
Verified Purchase

I'm being serious. It's the first time I ever do that. I've read tons of fantastic and game changing books, but it has been a while since I have read something that buffeted me on the face. I've failed 3 personal startups, (They all died in the MVP phase). Even though I did "customer discovery". I can't believe how biased I was when I was asking questions.

Legally speaking, I'd prefer if the pirated version wasn't there, since it has some implications on copyright and IP. And I've attempted

---

[44] You can see Hillman's self-hosted store page at: stackingthebricks.com/tinymba/, using IngramSpark to print and ship the physical copies.

several times to get the site owner to remove it. But given that he seems fairly determined to ignore me (and that I don't have a good way to track down the folks who are printing bootleg paperbacks in southeast Asia), let's examine the implications of your entire book being "stolen" and distributed for free.

Counterintuitively, recommendable books tend to benefit from piracy, since the folks who "steal" it will still end up recommending it to others who choose to pay. Plus, lots of the people who end up downloading the pirated version wouldn't have been able to get it otherwise (commonly due to a weak local currency). In which case, you can consider "piracy" to be a part of your social impact contribution.[45]

It is possible, however, to leverage piracy even further. This is accomplished by using the book as lead generation or deal flow for a broader business. As mentioned in the previous section about upsells, if you're running a full-service business like consulting or training, then your book has *far* more value as a source of lead generation than as a direct source of royalties.

Even if you're just building an audience or selling semi-related books and products, you still stand to benefit. You may have noticed that I'm doing this quite explicitly in this guide by finding the occasional excuse to mention my software for beta reading, my authors' community, my other content, and so on.

In general, the more revenue you receive from ongoing relationships with happy customers, the more excited you should be about book piracy. Whereas if your income comes primarily through the book royalties themselves, then you should be slightly more strategic.

In either case, I think it's best to assume your book will eventually be pirated. At which point, the question becomes: what hooks can you put into it (without withholding value or frustrating

---

[45] In some cases, you can even support this. I gave the rights for my Farsi translation (and a fair amount of my time) to an Iranian nonprofit that simply wanted to share the book's knowledge with local entrepreneurs. They've now distributed thousands of copies for which I'll never see a single cent, which is great. Worst case, I've helped some people who wouldn't have been able to buy the book otherwise. Best case, I've done that while *also* growing an audience who will recommend the book in the future.

your readers) that will allow even a "free" reader to end up helping you?

## Most authors ignore their fans, so you should engage with yours

In his influential essay *1,000 True Fans*[46], career creative Kevin Kelly observes:

> *Most creators in the last century did not have direct contact with consumers. Despite being in business for hundreds of years, no New York book publisher knew the names of their core and dedicated readers.*

That's still largely true, which creates an opportunity. Folks love being able to get in touch with an author, and engaging with those fans will help create both super-evangelists and marketing/PR opportunities.

But since Amazon controls the relationship and contact details of most of your customers,[47] you'll need to offer them both the ability and the motivation to get in touch with you.

The more "salesy" strategy — already discussed — is to offer a digital bonus (i.e., a lead magnet like an extra chapter, case study, or tools) on your site in exchange for a reader's email address and permission to contact them.

The second option is perhaps less "optimal" in terms of selling stuff, but has the benefit of being quick, easy, and authentic. All you need to do is to make yourself available when someone has a question or comment, and then spend a few minutes to reply. If you do that consistently, you'll amplify reader evangelism as well as serendipitous promotional opportunities.

---

[46] From Kelly's blog at kk.org: permanent.link/to/wub/1000-fans

[47] I'm generally quite positive about publishing through Amazon, but the one huge downside is being unable to directly reach out to happy customers to continue the relationship, or to unhappy customers to help when something goes wrong.

Your specific approach might be different, but I'll tell you how I do it. First and foremost, I share my contact details all over the place, and especially within the book itself (e.g., I'm rob@robfitz.com or @robfitz on Twitter). Second, I respond. Not always as quickly as I would like (sorry!), but I do try to get there eventually. And lastly, I keep an occasional eye on social media for mentions of my books, jumping into the conversation when it feels appropriate. That's it. And it has led to more opportunities than I can count.

Although social media is an ineffective use of time for outbound marketing (unless you happen to already have a large audience), it's the author's best friend for reader engagement and support. This doesn't require spending all day tweeting, nor even attempting to directly grow a following. Almost all reader contact can be inbound (i.e., they come to you or mention your book) instead of outbound (i.e., you say something clever that they react to).

I've recently been attempting to merge reader engagement with (finally) building an author platform. For the past few months, whenever a reader asks a question, instead of sending an email reply, I record the answer as a public video on my YouTube channel[48] and send them a link. This requires slightly more time, but doubles as a permanent piece of content to help build my fledgling audience. As we've already discussed, the "trick" of sustainable marketing is to find ways to integrate and overlap it with whatever you're already doing, and answering reader questions is a perfect fit for that.

You may also want to scan for mentions of your book from potentially influential fans, even if they don't directly message you. (You can do this most easily by setting up a Google Alert or running a Twitter search.) After someone has made a positive comment, send them a note to say hello and thanks. This takes very little time and can lead to plenty of positive opportunities and connections.

Some of my biggest podcast appearances came through this approach, where I said, "Hey, I saw you mentioned the book — big thanks and let me know if there's anything I can help with," and then they replied with some sort of splendid opportunity.

---

[48] Have a question? Ask and I'll answer with a video: youtube.com/c/robfitzpatrick

You won't be able to maintain this sort of personal service forever. But that's a problem for another day, once you're struggling under the weight of your own success. In the meantime, by building something useful and then remaining attentive and available to your audience, you allow good things to happen to you.

Once your book is working, it's worth optimizing, which includes:

1. The purchase funnel (primarily including your book cover, title/subtitle, store page, and reader reviews)
2. Adding percentage sales boosts (like extra platforms, formats, and related products)
3. Making the most of pricing, piracy, and paying attention to your fans

And with that all set and sorted, it's time for a final review of everything we've learned. (Plus some extra resources in the Appendix.)

# Conclusion and thanks

Most books require active, ongoing marketing to grow. However, a rare few are useful enough to benefit from strong word of mouth and timeless relevance, growing automatically year after year.

Instead of trying to figure out how to market whatever book you happened to write, a book can be intentionally designed and refined toward maximizing word of mouth and back-catalog potential.

You probably can't write the world's best book about a huge topic for every type of reader. Decide who you're serving and how you're helping them, and then write just for them. Better to be loved by someone than ignored by everyone.

Test your book with real readers, even before it has been written. Use listening and teaching conversations to build reader empathy, escape the curse of knowledge, and begin verifying the desirability of your book's promise and the effectiveness of its contents. Ensure that the book's knowledge can cross the air gap and make an impact on your readers.

Put it out there for feedback before it feels ready. Use beta readers. Fall in love with negative feedback. Iterate and improve.

While doing your beta reading, rewrites, and revisions, pay attention to the reader experience, which is defined as the pacing of value received over time spent. Add word counts to a detailed, descriptive ToC to visualize and debug that reader experience.

Engagement and recommendability both rely on readers rapidly extracting significant value from the text. As such, the book should be as short as possible and its value should be front-loaded. Don't get stuck in theory and don't delay the big reveal. This also boosts the book's value-per-page and keeps a reader reading.

Pay attention to where beta readers are giving up and drifting away — their disengagement is evidence of either confusion or boredom. Put extra effort into improving the surrounding sections and chapters.

To begin growing through word of mouth, you must manually create a seed audience via some mix of one-off marketing efforts such as PPC ads, event giveaways, the digital/podcast book tour, and writing in public.

Once your book is already selling, you can optimize and accelerate your growth by fixing the funnel, adding percentage sales boosts by offering extra formats and support, and engaging with your fans.

While this approach could be used by both traditionally published and self-published authors, it's especially valuable for those interested in maximizing long-term passive income via self-publishing.

That's it. Hope it was useful. (And let me know if not so I can improve it.)

## Acknowledgements

Infinite appreciation to Teresa Fradera and Devin Hunt, my life and business partners, respectively. Looking forward to seeing what we get up to together over the next few decades.

Huge thanks to Veronica Torras, who nudged me into writing this book by asking for a bit of advice about her own, and who shaped its foundations as my very first reader conversation and beta reader. And to Adam M. Rosen, my editor. I'm hard enough to work with once, so I appreciate you sticking around for another round.

Unending gratitude to all early readers and supporters — far too numerous to name — who have offered time, insights, interviews, beta reading, feedback, and encouragement. I learned so much from all of you and I loved every minute of it.

And to my mom, Diana, whose unconditional support allowed me to get started on this whole meandering journey.

## Thanks

I really appreciate you taking the leap, grabbing this guide, and spending your time with it.

While I'm aware that my approach to book-making is slightly unusual and won't be right for everyone, I hope that at least some small piece of it can help your book to receive more of the attention, audience, and impact it deserves.

Shoot me a note sometime and let me know how you get on with your book. I'd like to hear about it.

Wishing you all the very best,
Rob Fitzpatrick

# Appendix

## Resources and contact

Beta reading tool: helpthisbook.com (built by Devin and myself and used for the beta reading of this book)

Nonfiction authors' community: writeusefulbooks.com/community/

Author interviews and extra learning:

- April Dunford on the year-long launch: writeusefulbooks.com/dunford/
- Tendayi Viki on finding the tone and time: writeusefulbooks.com/viki/
- Arvid Kahl on writing in public to build an author platform: writeusefulbooks.com/kahl/
- And many more: writeusefulbooks.com/resources

My videos: youtube.com/c/robfitzpatrick (ask a question and I'll answer with a little video)

My other writing: robfitz.com (my books, some essays, and a sporadic newsletter of whatever is holding my attention)

Me: rob@robfitz.com or @robfitz

# Tutorials and tool walkthroughs

I wrote several extra chapters on the step-by-step practicalities of the tasks of self-publishing, printing, advertising, picking the right tools, and more.

However, since these topics all rely on fast-changing software, including them in the book would risk misleading you with outdated information. So I'm instead maintaining them as digital guides, which I will update as the tools change.

You can access them for free (no email or signup required):

- Navigating KDP set-up options: writeusefulbooks.com/guides/kdp-faq/
- Setting up your first Amazon ads: writeusefulbooks.com/guides/ppc/
- Bulk paperback printing: writeusefulbooks.com/guides/bulk-printing/
- Interior page layout for all formats: writeusefulbooks.com/guides/layout/

Any other guides added in the future will be at: writeusefulbooks.com/guides/

# Self-publishing checklist

For the latest version of this checklist: writeusefulbooks.com/guides/selfpub/

Copyediting to strengthen the prose:

- Copy editors help tremendously with clarity, conciseness, and phrasing, but don't deal with big-picture structural issues, so ensure that you've already sorted all that out via beta reading and/or developmental editing

- $500+ to hire a freelancer, based on word count (strongly recommended if possible, since doing it yourself is *extremely* time-consuming and will never be as good as what a professional can provide)

Final review readers to cover any gaps left by beta reading, potentially including:

- Influential readers to gather pre-launch testimonials for the book's cover and the "editorial reviews" section on your Amazon page
- Expert readers to check for inaccuracies and overgeneralizations
- Sensitivity readers to catch unintentional bias, insensitivity, and marginalization
- A legal review (normally only relevant if you're worried about potential libel or IP issues from using anecdotes/quotes of real people or entities, but mandatory if you intend to insure the book as a business asset)

Proofreading to fix typos and grammar, thereby finalizing the manuscript:

- $150+ to hire a freelancer (highly recommended — terrific value for money in terms of time and sanity saved)
- Traditionally, proofreaders work from the formatted PDF of your semi-final book in order to catch layout errors — but I prefer to have them work directly in my manuscript doc (far faster to integrate the suggestions) and then take responsibility for verifying page layouts myself

Interior page layouts for paperback, ebook, and (optionally) PDF:

- Worth learning yourself if you intend to make frequent updates, but otherwise freelancers are readily available at great rates

- If your book requires an index, glossary, or fancy layout/typography, then freelance help becomes both more important and more expensive
- If doing it yourself, you're (currently) stuck choosing between "easy and beautiful but inflexible" (Vellum, Reedsy, Kindle Create, etc.), or "fiddly and tedious but customizable" (MS Word with a book template, Google Docs with add-ons[49], Adobe InDesign, etc.)
- After it has been exported, always scan each page of the final PDF for weird page breaks: the first/last line of a list or paragraph dangling on a separate page, section headings that begin as a page ends, illustrations getting displaced and leaving lots of whitespace, and so on

Create cover images:

- Front cover for ebook, front/back/spine for paperback (leave an empty corner for the ISBN and barcode on the back of the paperback), and a square version for the audiobook (if you have one)
- Use an online calculator for paperback spine width once you know your page count, paper weight, and book dimensions
- $50-500 to hire a freelancer if desired (or fairly reasonable DIY templates are a Google search away)

Decide how to do your print-on-demand and where to sell your books:

- If selling through Amazon, do it all via Amazon KDP ("Kindle Direct Publishing") which, despite its name, also handles paperbacks (see Chapter 8 for optimizations and the Appendix for guidance on setup options)

---

[49] I ended up using Google Docs for the entire layout of this book, including the versions for print, PDF, and ebook. Doing so does require a couple add-ons and extra tools, but it's a surprisingly viable option. Plus, it's free. Full guide at: writeusefulbooks.com/guides/layout/

- If setting up your own website and storefront, use IngramSpark + Shopify to handle everything (i.e., selling, printing, and shipping) — this requires being fairly comfortable with multiple tech tools, although no actual coding is required

Get some ISBNs, which are your book's identification number and barcode:

- The simple option is to accept the free ISBNs from either Amazon or IngramSpark (which they'll offer to you while setting up your book), but doing so does carry some limitations and restrictions that are worth researching (I did this for my first two books and it was fine, but I'm using the next option for this book)
- The more professional option is to buy your own ISBNs and "publish" the book under your own publishing imprint — this is relatively straightforward if you already have a business entity, but requires setting one up if not, which obviously carries an accounting and admin burden
- You'll use a different ISBN for each format (e.g., hardback, paperback, Kindle, iBooks, etc.) and each new version (only for major updates, minor fixes don't matter)

That's a big list that potentially includes a few new tasks you didn't even know existed. But although many of these tasks are indeed a bit fiddly and tedious, they're also fairly predictable, solvable, and low-risk. You can do them. A million titles are self-published per year, many by first time authors. Plus, all sorts of helpful blog posts, tutorials, and guides have been written by the folks who have already been through it.

# Okay that's it

Thanks again for your support.

You can find me at rob@robfitz.com or @robfitz on Twitter. My other books and projects are linked via robfitz.com.

writeusefulbooks.com

Printed in Great Britain
by Amazon

70394415R00081